Armies of the Viking Age
840–1100
History, Organisation and Equipment

GABRIELE ESPOSITO

HISTORIC ARMIES SERIES, VOLUME 4

Gabriele Esposito
Gabriele Esposito is a military historian who works as a freelance author and researcher for the military history sector. He specialises in uniformology, and his interests and expertise range from ancient civilisations to modern post-colonial conflicts. During recent years, he has conducted several lines of research on the military history of non-European countries. His books and essays are published on a regular basis internationally. He is also the author of numerous military history articles.

Acknowledgements
This book is dedicated to my beloved parents, Maria Rosaria and Benedetto. A very special thanks to Key Publishing for believing in my editorial projects and for precious support. A very special mention goes to the brilliant reenactment groups that collaborated with me so that their photographs could be used in the creation of this book: without their research, this publication would not have been the same. My deep gratitude to the following living history associations: Hrafn Vaeringi and Stronghold Re-enactment from the United Kingdom, Compagnie de la Branche Rouge and Vigamadr from France, The Skjaldborg from the USA, Taillefer from Germany, and Gunnar from the Czech Republic.

Published by Key Books
An imprint of Key Publishing Ltd
PO Box 100
Stamford
Lincs PE9 1XQ

www.keypublishing.com

The right of Gabriele Esposito to be identified as the author of this book has been asserted in accordance with the Copyright, Designs and Patents Act 1988 Sections 77 and 78.

Copyright © Gabriele Esposito, 2024

ISBN 978 1 80282 793 4

All rights reserved. Reproduction in whole or in part in any form whatsoever or by any means is strictly prohibited without the prior permission of the Publisher.

Typeset by SJmagic DESIGN SERVICES, India.

Contents

Introduction 4
Chapter 1 The Rise of the Vikings 6
Chapter 2 The Vikings in England 10
Chapter 3 Viking England 24
Chapter 4 Harald Hardrada 28
Chapter 5 William of Normandy 34
Chapter 6 The Vikings in the Celtic Nations 43
Chapter 7 The Birth of Normandy 60
Chapter 8 The Viking Settlement of the Atlantic 74
Chapter 9 The Vikings in Eastern Europe 84
Chapter 10 The End of the Viking World 94
Chapter 11 Viking Military Organisation 103
Chapter 12 Viking Military Equipment and Tactics 111
Bibliography 124
Contributors 125

Introduction

The Vikings are some of the most significant peoples of the Middle Ages. Their ferocious raids and rapid incursions into non-native lands to plunder portable wealth and carry away people into slavery is part of their acknowledged identity and a facet of their character for which they are known more than a millennium later. The Vikings were much more than simple raiders who terrorised much of medieval Europe, however. They were navigators and explorers with incredible skills, crossing oceans and the rivers of the Northern Hemisphere in search of new lands in which to settle and live in prosperity.

Viking expansionism and migrations involved large portions of the known world in the central centuries of the Middle Ages. From their homeland in southern Scandinavia, Vikings settled in the British Isles before advancing further west. They reached Iceland and Greenland after crossing the Atlantic Ocean and populated these islands. From their new outposts, Scandinavian explorers moved further west, reaching the coastline of present-day Canada and establishing a short-lived settlement in North America known as Vinland.

In practice, the Vikings were the first Europeans to live in the Americas and the first navigators to understand the potential of the Atlantic Ocean, which had once been revered as the 'edge of the world' by ancient civilisations.

The Viking presence in Britain and Ireland was characterised by continuous conflict with local populations, who saw Scandinavian newcomers as deadly rivals. In Britain, after decades of incessant fighting with the Saxons, the Vikings created their own short-lived domain known as the Danelaw. In Ireland, they were utterly defeated by the local Celtic communities after gaining control of large portions of the island. To the east of Scotland, however, the Vikings were able to establish a long-lasting realm known as the Kingdom of the Isles, which comprised the Hebrides, the Isle of Man and the islands of the Firth of Clyde. This realm existed until the mid-13th century and was a long-lasting presence on the political scene of the British Isles. During their era, the Vikings exerted control over the Orkney and Shetland islands, to the point where their influence over the peripheral areas of Britain was significant.

In Western Europe, Scandinavian explorers and conquerors also had other targets within their sights, most notably the territories of the former Frankish Empire (current-day areas of France, Belgium and Germany). Territorial unity had been lost among the Franks soon after the death of its founder Charlemagne, and consequently it was easy prey for the Vikings. Normandy and Brittany in Northern France were also frequently raided and ravaged. The newly born kingdom of France was unable to counter these advances in an effective way, which resulted in the famous Viking siege of Paris (845). In order to save the central regions of their kingdom, the French monarchs ceded Normandy to Scandinavian pirates. In their new French homeland, the Vikings flourished and gradually evolved into feudal aristocrats. However, they never lost their original spirit of conquest and during the following decades moved from Normandy to conquer England and southern Italy. The warriors who won at Hastings in 1066 and who conquered southern Italy during the early 11th century, however, were quite different from their Viking ancestors. They were not sea raiders armed with axes; they were feudal knights with training and discipline. Before long, the Vikings of Normandy had reshaped their self-image and started to be known as Normans.

Introduction

In Eastern Europe, where they were known as Varangians, the Vikings obtained incredible results in a very short time. From Sweden, they moved into Estonia and Finland before exploring settlements along the great Russian rivers. Over decades, they colonised much of present-day Russia and Ukraine, subjugating the local tribes of Slavs and establishing the first centralised realm in that region of Europe: the immense Grand Principality of Kievan Rus', stretching from Novgorod on the Baltic Sea to the Black Sea in southern Ukraine. Russia, or the Land of the Rus, was dominated by a Varangian elite, which was strong enough to menace the Byzantine Empire from the north. Like their French equivalents, the Byzantine monarchs had to reach a compromise with the Scandinavians in order to retain their realms: they sent large amounts of gold to the Grand Principality of Kievan Rus' and created a strong military corps of mercenary Scandinavians that became known as the Varangian Guard. It became part of the Byzantine Imperial Guard and soon earned the reputation of a legendary combat corps.

This book describes the most important military campaigns fought by the Vikings and analyses their military organisation as well as their traditional weapons. The analysis begins with the first Viking invasion of Britain in 840 and ends at the year 1100. Gradually, over the course of the 11th century, the Vikings of Scandinavia lost most of their distinctive characteristics, adopting the Christian faith and feudal organisation of society almost simultaneously. Denmark, Norway and Sweden were all organised as proper kingdoms and the traditions of the Vikings were gradually marginalised. In Eastern Europe, the situation was different since Kievan Rus' continued to flourish until it later fractured into smaller states due to its internal divisions. Despite these changes, the Scandinavian nations of Denmark, Norway and Sweden have always retained some distinctive Viking character and that is still seen today. The same can be said for Iceland and Greenland, two islands that were populated by the Vikings and with a mostly Scandinavian culture.

Chapter 1
The Rise of the Vikings

The terms Vikings and Varangians are commonly used to identify the Scandinavian raiders who operated across Europe during 800–1000AD. All Vikings belonged to a larger group of Norsemen. These were a north Germanic ethno-linguistic group that spoke the Old Norse language and lived in the southern part of Scandinavia. Their homeland comprised present-day Denmark and the southern parts of Norway and Sweden. From a cultural point of view, the Norsemen had a lot in common with the South Germanic tribes who invaded the Roman Empire during the last centuries of Antiquity (pre 5th century). The Norsemen differed from the southern Germani, however, in having had very little contact with more advanced civilisations such as the Celts or the Romans. As a result, the material culture of the Norsemen was 'primitive' compared to the more advanced Europeans from the Mediterranean region.

Like the earlier South Germanic tribes, the Norsemen were skilled warriors and lived in small rural villages. They knew how to work metals to produce formidable weapons. They did not practice agriculture on a very large scale. Their lands were difficult to reach for foreign merchants, and the natural environment in which they lived was particularly harsh. Their economy was very simple, without a monetary system. During the long centuries of the Roman Empire, their only direct contact with the regions of southern Europe was the commerce of amber, a precious material that could be found in the Baltic Sea. The Norsemen knew very little of the rest of the world and were too few to represent a driving force in the new world emerging from Antiquity.

Over time, however, the situation started to change rapidly and an increasing number of Norsemen began to leave their homeland to travel abroad in search of new lands to raid or colonise. Those Norsemen who traded their lifestyle to become pirates and explorers started to be known as Vikings or Varangians; so, it's true to say that all Vikings were Norsemen but only some Norsemen were Vikings. The expansion of the Norsemen across northern Europe began during the last decades of the eighth century, in an age that saw the ascendancy of the Frankish Empire in Continental Europe and the end of Arab expansionism across the Mediterranean.

Before the beginning of the Viking Age, southern Scandinavia experienced a great demographic expansion. Until the first half of the 8th century, the climate of Denmark and Norway limited agricultural production significantly and was therefore too cold to support the existence of a large population. By 750, the climate had become less cold and the population started to grow when the production of food supplies increased. Over a few decades, the demographic situation of Scandinavia changed to the point where the region began experiencing problems of overpopulation. The agricultural capacity of the land was now inadequate to keep up with the increasing population and many Norsemen were without the means of providing themselves with sustenance. The number of individuals who had no land or personal property expanded, especially once all cultivable lands were occupied. The sudden demographic boom produced landless men who were in search of material wealth in order to feed their families, or of new territories on which to settle as farmers. These individuals left their homeland in search of new opportunities, operating as pirates or crossing the seas as explorers. Unlike the southern Germanic communities, the Norsemen were skilled navigators and knew how to build the most effective ships; travelling long distances across the ocean or following the course of rivers for hundreds of miles was their skill set.

Several other changes took place in Scandinavia during the 8th century. First of all, iron became more common as new mines from which this important material could be extracted were discovered and opened. Increasing amounts of iron were used to produce more effective weapons as well as new agricultural tools that increased the productivity of Norse farmers. In addition, the Norsemen improved their seafaring capabilities by perfecting the design and engineering of their ships. Larger sails were introduced, together with new practices for arranging them. These innovations, together with the ability to sail at night by following the stars, enabled Norsemen to plan ambitious raids and expeditions.

When the Viking Age began, there was no centralised government in Denmark, Sweden and Norway. Each tribal group had a supreme leader but there was no political entity that could control Viking expansionism from a central point. All the Norsemen were pagans and the Christian faith was not yet practised north of Charlemagne's domains. When the Vikings started launching their raids, their primary target in the west was the British Isles, since most of Continental Europe was under the firm military control of the Carolingians. The Carolingians had a very strong military apparatus and a centralised administration that could defend its territory in an effective way. The military and political situation of Britain and Ireland was completely different and was characterised by widespread fragmentation. England was populated by the Anglo-Saxons, a people who had crossed the Channel some centuries before and who had created their own small realms in the region after crushing the resistance of the Romano-British communities.

A Viking warrior equipped with sword and round shield. (© Skjaldborg Vikings)

For several decades, until Alfred the Great unified the country in 886, England was divided into seven small kingdoms that were constantly at war with each other. Collectively known as the 'Heptarchy', these kingdoms comprised East Anglia, Mercia, Northumbria, Wessex, Essex, Kent and Sussex. These areas do not correspond to the modern areas of England bearing the same names, and were much larger with variable boundaries. The Vikings were aware that the Britain was weak militarily if each area was attacked singularly and they nurtured the ambition of conquering the whole territory of England one day. England was a rich land, full of natural resources and perfect for agriculture. By conquering that nation, the Scandinavians would resolve their problems of overpopulation in their native lands.

To the west of Anglo-Saxon England were the small Celtic realms of Wales, which had been able to stop the expansionism of the Saxons during the previous decades, but which were too fragmented politically to represent a significant military entity. Around 780, there were five main princedoms in Wales: Gwynedd, Powys, Dyfed, Gwent and Dumnonia. These were all inhabited by the direct heirs of the Romano-British communities who fought against the Saxons in England and had a distinctive culture.

A Viking warrior wearing a Gjermundbu helmet. (Photo Gunnar, © Dominika Černá)

To the north of the Heptarchy was Scotland, which had been inhabited by a confederation of Celtic peoples known as Picts. They had been at war with the Romans for a long time and launched devastating raids across England. The leading group among the Picts was the Fortriu, which dominated other minor communities. However, there were two smaller and independent kingdoms in the territory of present-day western Scotland that were not controlled by the Picts: the kingdom of Dál Riata and the kingdom of Strathclyde. The former was inhabited by Scoti coming from Ireland, while the latter was populated by Britons who had much in common with the Celtic communities of Wales.

When compared with the Anglo-Saxons of England, however, the Picts were less fragmented politically since they controlled most of Scotland. Ireland was inhabited by the Scoti or Gaels, another confederation of Celtic peoples who had a lot in common with the Picts. Over time the original alliance between the Scoti and the Picts was destroyed by internal rivalries. The establishment of the kingdom of Dál Riata in western Scotland led to several conflicts between the two communities. The Scoti of Ireland were extremely fragmented politically, since their clans were organised as independent princedoms and were constantly at war with each other.

There were six small realms in Ireland by the beginning of the Viking raids: Munster, Leinster, Connacht, Airgialla, Uí Néill and Ulaid. Like the Anglo-Saxon states of the Heptarchy, these were frequently ravaged by civil wars and sometimes one of them emerged as a regional power.

Chapter 2
The Vikings in England

Lindisfarne

The first Vikings appeared in England in 789, when three of their ships sailed to the Isle of Portland in Dorset. These Scandinavian sailors were mistaken for merchants by a local royal official and were asked to pay a trading tax on the goods that they were transporting. Offended by the request of the local authorities, the Scandinavians murdered the royal official and left the island. This early episode of Viking violence in England may have been the result of an explorative mission but the attitude continued over future expeditions. The real starting point of the Viking raids against England, however, is marked by a famous attack against the Holy Island of Lindisfarne in 793. Located off the coast of Northumbria, Lindisfarne was one of the most important religious sites of Anglo-Saxon England: its monastery was extremely rich and its monastic community exerted a strong influence over north-eastern England. The Vikings knew that the island/monastery was full of treasures and were aware that Lindisfarne could be attacked easily from the sea.

The Scandinavians landed without encountering opposition and took the local community by surprise. Being pagan, they showed no respect for the monks and killed everyone they encountered in their pursuit. The whole Christian world was shocked by the events that took place at Lindisfarne: a group of violent 'pagan devils' had razed to the ground a holy monastery after killing many monks and civilians in order to steal the treasures that were preserved in a peaceful religious site. The events of 793 had an enormous psychological impact over the inhabitants of Northumbria: a new deadly menace was now on the horizon for England and the Anglo-Saxon kingdoms were unprepared to face it.

A Viking warrior armed with spear and sword.
(© Vigamadr)

Tynemouth

In 794, a small Viking fleet attacked the rich monastery of Jarrow in Northumbria. This time, the raiders encountered strong resistance and some of their leaders were killed during the fight. Unexpectedly, they were forced to leave without capturing treasures or slaves. Following their defeat, the Scandinavian raiders had their ships beached at Tynemouth and were all massacred by local people who had been alerted by the attack on Jarrow. Unlike the success of 793, this second Viking expedition against a monastery in England had been a total failure: the Scandinavians had attacked with a very limited number of men and had been blocked by the strong resistance of the locals. In addition, they had suffered from a lack of knowledge of the coastline along which they were operating and had been slaughtered following the failure of their assault.

These first two Viking attacks in England illustrate that the Scandinavian raiders in this early phase of their evolution preferred to assault isolated religious sites where they could plunder transportable goods and capture slaves without encountering any serious resistance. This strategy allowed them to conduct their expeditions with a very limited number of ships. Following the raid against Jarrow, the Vikings continued to attack English objectives but infrequently. Monasteries and minster churches remained their favoured targets, since they contained valuable objects that could easily be transported away.

During these years, the Vikings started to direct their incursions against Scotland and Ireland. They knew that they could pillage England, but to do that they needed to organise their incursions in an effective military and logistical way. In 840, the Scandinavians organised a new expedition against England, with the primary target being the Kingdom of Wessex. This time the raiders assembled a large army that was made up of several bands of Vikings and which was transported on a total of 35 ships. The Vikings had learned that small expeditions involving just a few ships could achieve very limited results and only for a very short time.

A Viking warrior equipped with short-sleeved chainmail. (Photo Gunnar, © Dominika Černá)

Batte of Carhampton

Aethelwulf, monarch of Wessex, moved against the Vikings at the head of his army but was defeated after three days of bloody fighting at the Battle of Carhampton (Somerset). This was the first major pitched clash fought in England between the Scandinavians and the Saxons, and the first important victory obtained by the Vikings outside their homeland.

After defeating Aethelwulf, the pirates were free to plunder Somerset for several days without meeting any serious opposition, killing hundreds of people and capturing many slaves. The Vikings often conducted their incursions to capture young people who could work on their behalf in the Scandinavian fields. This knowledge increased the terror of the local Saxon communities who lived in areas exposed to Viking raids. During the years 840–860, Scandinavian raiders continued to attack the Kingdom of Wessex, since its military resources had been greatly damaged. Aethelwulf, however, gradually learned how to deal with the Viking raids and was able to repulse several after achieving some minor victories. Sporadic Scandinavian attacks against England continued during 840–860, but the Battle of Carhampton had shown that the Saxon realms were weak, so the pirates changed their strategy and abandoned the practice of conducting small local incursions in favour of organising larger invasions.

The Great Heathen Army

Around 860, the Viking war leaders who had conducted raids in England assembled their forces into a large fleet, with which they could invade a portion of the Saxon lands. The new military force organised by the Vikings soon became known as the 'Great Heathen Army' in England; it comprised several thousand warriors and was mostly made up of Danes as well as raiders from Norway and Sweden. Instead of landing in Wessex, as they had done several times during the previous decades, the leaders of the Great Heathen Army chose to attack East Anglia and Kent.

The long-planned Scandinavian invasion of England took place in 865, after several minor attacks that were conducted against the kingdom of Northumbria. The Great Heathen Army landed on the Isle of Thanet, which was soon transformed into an important operational base for the Vikings; the people of Kent tried to find a compromise with the newcomers, by offering them the payment of a special tribute (which became known as 'danegeld') in exchange for peace.

The Vikings did not accept any form of payment and started to pillage the eastern portion of Kent with brutal violence. Following these events, the Kingdom of East Anglia decided to arrange terms with the foreign invaders who had by now established a permanent base in Kent. In exchange for horses and food, the Vikings did not ravage the territory of East Anglia; here they spent the winter of 865–866 before moving north to invade the kingdom of Northumbria. The military forces of Northumbria were easily defeated by the Scandinavians, who obtained danegeld from the local population and even placed their own 'puppet' monarch on the throne of Northumbria.

A Viking warrior armed with spear, sword and seax short sabre. (© Compagnie de la Branche Rouge)

After building up a new important base at York, the Vikings moved against the kingdom of Mercia where they captured Nottingham during 867. Burgred, monarch of Mercia, soon understood that he had no choice but to form an alliance with the kingdom of Wessex in order to repulse the Great Heathen Army. Wessex, in fact, was too strong to be defeated by a single Saxon army. The combined military forces of Mercia and Wessex besieged Nottingham for some time, but did not achieve any significant result. As a result, Burgred surrendered and agreed to pay the danegeld to the Vikings. During 868–869 the Great Heathen Army remained in York after having defeated Kent, East Anglia, Northumbria and Mercia. During the first months of 870, however, hostilities resumed between the Scandinavians and East Anglia. The king of East Anglia, Edmund, did his best to stop the expansion of the foreigners. A series of bloody battles were fought between Edmund and the Vikings, all of which he lost. The English monarch was captured and tortured before being killed, thus leaving East Anglia open for Scandinavian settlement.

Above left: **A Viking warrior carrying a throwing javelin and sword.** (© **Skjaldborg Vikings**)

Above right: **A Viking spearman. Note the complex decoration painted on the shield.**
(© **Compagnie de la Branche Rouge**)

The Great Summer Army

In the summer of 871, a new Viking army, known as the Great Summer Army, consisting of several thousands of warriors, landed in England to secure the Scandinavian possessions in the region. With the arrival of these reinforcements, the Vikings turned their attention to the Kingdom of Wessex, which was now ruled by Aethelred, who could count on the support of his younger brother Alfred.

On 8 January 871, the Battle of Ashdown took place in Berkshire between the Vikings and the Saxons of Wessex. The clash took place on a location that was chosen by the Scandinavian warriors, who selected high ground for themselves. During the battle, Alfred, the future 'Alfred the Great', showed all his courage and his great military capabilities. He launched a violent frontal attack against the dominant positions of the enemy, crushing the Viking line after some very harsh fighting. The Scandinavians suffered heavy losses during the battle and were followed in close pursuit by Alfred during the following night. The important success obtained by the Saxons at Ashdown arrested the Viking pursuit for some time and saved Wessex from destruction, but it was not a decisive victory. After a few weeks, the Scandinavians resumed their offensive and obtained two minor victories at Basing and Meretun. Three months after the Battle of Ashdown, Alfred became King of Wessex following the sudden death of his brother. The new monarch, after having been defeated at Basing and Meretun, was in no condition to continue the fight against the foreign invaders, who outnumbered his own forces.

Alfred the Great

To reorganise his military forces and to forge new alliances with other English kings, Alfred needed time. He paid large sums of money to the Vikings in order to suspend the hostilities and save his realm from the devastation of war. With their campaign in Wessex complete, the Scandinavians became heavily involved in Northumbria, where they went to crush a rebellion of the local population. The locals were easily suppressed and the Vikings were able to restore their puppet ruler on the throne of Northumbria. Over time, the Scandinavian presence in England became a stable one, since the Vikings could exert direct or indirect control over four of the major Anglo-Saxon kingdoms. A new sense of 'national' unity, however, was developing among the remaining English communities thanks to the brilliant leadership of Alfred. The Saxons, in fact, were becoming aware that only by uniting all their military resources could they expel the Vikings from their country.

In 874, the Scandinavians chose to occupy Mercia and expelled the local monarch. From here, the Vikings divided their large military forces into two parts. One marched north from Northumbria and went to Scotland in order to pillage as much as possible. The other established a new operational base at Cambridge in view of new expansionist moves. Initially Alfred of Wessex tried to maintain peaceful relations with the Scandinavians, but his attempts were unsuccessful. During 875–878, the Great Heathen Army raided a large portion of Wessex, causing serious losses to the local population and devastating much of the countryside. To save his military forces and gain more time for preparation, Alfred went to the inhospitable Marsh of Athelney in Somerset, where he was protected from the attacks of the enemy by the harsh nature of the local terrain. After having reorganised his troops, Alfred finally gave battle at Edington in Wiltshire. The decisive clash took place in May 878 and saw the confrontation between the monarch of Wessex and the Viking leader Guthrum the Old. Few details are known about the Battle of Edington, but it surely started with a massive Scandinavian attack that was repulsed by the Saxons (who deployed themselves in a strong defensive formation). The Viking assault was crushed and was followed by a violent counter-attack that decided the outcome of the clash in favour of Alfred the Great. The Vikings suffered heavy losses and their few survivors were surrounded by Saxons. The Scandinavians had suffered their first serious defeat in England after decades of victorious raids. They sued for peace and sent several hostages to Alfred with the promise that they would abandon the territory of Wessex immediately.

Three weeks after the Battle of Edington, Guthrum was baptised, with Alfred as his sponsor. Some time later, the Vikings abandoned Wessex and retreated to their bases in East Anglia where they remained quiet. A peace treaty was signed between the two parties, according to which Alfred was recognised by the Vikings as the overlord of the Saxons while the Scandinavian presence in England was recognised as a legitimate one by Alfred. This was the first fundamental step towards the formation of Danelaw, the Viking state of eastern England.

In 879, new military reinforcements arrived from Scandinavia, as a result of the Saxon victory at Edington. It was intended that the newcomers would resume the hostilities against Alfred, while Guthrum had no reasons to fight, at least for the moment. The newly arrived Viking contingents conducted sporadic raids against the borders of Wessex, but Alfred repelled these easily, thanks to the construction of some new fortified positions known as burhs. By 885, the internal divisions existing among the Vikings of England became deeper, since the newcomers settled in the northern portion of Danelaw while Guthrum ruled East Anglia as a proper king who was recognised by Alfred the Great. In 886, the rulers of Wessex and East Anglia signed an important treaty, defining conclusively the border separating their two kingdoms. The Kingdom of Mercia was partitioned between Alfred and Guthrum: the western portion was given to Wessex, and the eastern one was given to East Anglia. During the last years of his rule, Alfred was able to expand his realm and to reconquer (temporarily) York from the Vikings. The diplomatic relations between Wessex and East Anglia, however, remained positive until his death in 899. Alfred had been able to stop

A Viking warrior armed with a two-handed Danish axe. Note the excellent manufacture of his sword and seax. (Skjaldborg Vikings, © Darling Muse Photography)

the Vikings in their conquest of England and had unified all the Saxon territories that had not been conquered by the Scandinavians under his rule. By 900, the political situation of England had changed dramatically. The Heptarchy was no longer in existence, since Wessex and Danelaw controlled the whole territory of the country: East Anglia was in Viking hands, Mercia had been partitioned between Wessex and East Anglia, Northumbria was a Scandinavian protectorate, Essex was part of East Anglia and Kent was part of Wessex as well as Sussex. In practice, Alfred the Great had been able to unify most of southern and eastern England while the Vikings still controlled northern and western England.

Edward

After the death of Alfred, a civil war ravaged the newly unified Saxon Kingdom, since two rivals fought for the throne. Edward, elder son of Alfred, and Aethelwold, younger son of Aethelred. The second pretender was much weaker than the first one, since he could not count on the support of the most important Saxon aristocrats. As a result, Aethelwold decided to form a military alliance with the Vikings of Northumbria in order to count on the support of their warriors. The Saxon civil war came to an end in 903, when the Vikings of Northumbria were defeated decisively by Edward after having ravaged most of Mercia. Aethelwold and his main Viking ally were killed in battle and thus the elder son of Alfred the Great could finally consolidate his power.

After some years of relative peace, the hostilities between Edward and the Northumbrian Vikings resumed, leading to the Battle of Tettenhall in 910. It was a significant victory for the Saxons, who caused heavy losses to the Vikings before reconquering those areas of Mercia that had been lost previously.

While these events took place in England, the Scandinavians transformed Brittany into their main base on Continental Europe and from there they started to launch destructive incursions into southern England. Edward did his best to repulse these attacks and built a new defensive system of forts across his realm. After defeating Viking incursions from the sea and extending his political influence over southern Wales, the Saxon monarch resumed hostilities against Danelaw with the objective of claiming some border lands from East Anglia. During 917, thanks to a brilliant military campaign that was made up of sieges and counter-sieges, Edward was able to reduce the Viking presence in England. The whole central and southern portion of Danelaw was conquered by the Saxons and the Vikings remained in possession of just a few territories in Northumbria.

Meanwhile, in Scandinavia, the political situation was changing very rapidly. The Danish Vikings, who had been the main driving force behind the victories of the Great Heathen Army, were evolving. A first centralised Danish Kingdom was organised under the rule of Gorm the Old (936–958) and the Christian faith was introduced into the realm under the rule of Harald Bluetooth (958–986). As a result of these important changes, the number of Danish warriors willing to spend their life as raiders decreased progressively.

Around 918, a group of Norwegian Vikings, who had been raiding Ireland, conquered Northumbria from the Danes and occupied the city of York. As a result of these events, the Danish presence in England came to an end since both East Anglia and Essex had been conquered by Edward a few years before. The Norwegian Vikings continued to control a significant portion of Northumbria for several decades, despite being constantly

A housecarl (professional warrior) of Cnut the Great, equipped with nasal helmet and Danish axe. (Guljara Photography, © Stronghold Re-enactment)

at war with the Saxon Kingdom. The Scandinavian positions in England, however, became increasingly precarious since the unified Saxons could deploy significant military resources in the field. In 927, the Vikings were expelled from York and some years later most of Northumbria was temporarily occupied by the Saxons. Around 940, however, the Vikings were able to reconquer part of their Northumbrian territories, thanks to the decisive help of the Scandinavian raiders based in Ireland and to the arrival of some new reinforcements coming from Norway. A new Viking war leader, Olaf of York, emerged and organised a major offensive directed against central England, with the objective of reconquering the territories of the former Danelaw.

In 942, after some initial difficulties, the Saxons reorganised their military forces and repulsed the Viking offensive after reconquering all the lands that had been occupied by the Scandinavians. The Viking realm in Northumbria survived for just another few years, since the continuous wars with the Saxons and the revolts of the local population eventually caused its fall in 954. The Norwegian project of a Viking kingdom stretching from York to Dublin had failed and the last Scandinavian footholds in England had been destroyed after a century of Viking presence on the territory of the Saxon kingdoms.

A housecarl of Cnut the Great, wearing chainmail and nasal helmet. (© Skjaldborg Vikings)

Aethelred II

The fall of Danelaw and Northumbria, however, did not mark the end of the Viking raids in England: these continued during the following years, since the Scandinavians never abandoned their ambition of conquering the country. The reign of the Saxon monarch Aethelred II (978–1013) saw a series of new Viking attacks against England, which had the form of raids but were conducted by significant numbers of warriors. In August 991, a force of 4,000 Vikings, under command of the expert Olaf Tryggvason, disembarked at Maldon near the Blackwater River in Essex. The Scandinavians sailed up the river while the local Saxon forces organised themselves to face the threat represented by the newcomers. Byrhtnoth, Ealdorman of Essex, had a limited number of professional forces under his command to stop the Vikings and mobilised every able-bodied man of the region.

The Scandinavians stopped at an island placed in the middle of the Blackwater River and waited for the arrival of the enemy army. Initially, Olaf Tryggvason tried to find a compromise with the Saxons, promising them that he would have left England if his invasion force had been paid with large amounts of gold. Byrhtnoth, however, refused the offer and prepared his warriors for battle. A small land bridge connected the island where the Vikings were stationed to the nearby banks of the river and thus the Saxons had the opportunity to defend this narrow passage with a limited number of men. The accounts that we have of the battle are not precise, but what we know is that the Scandinavians were able to move their main force to the banks of the river and to deploy it in

A housecarl of Cnut the Great, equipped with short-sleeved chainmail. (Guljara Photography, © Stronghold Re-enactment)

combat formation. The ensuing fight was particularly violent and with many warriors killed on both sides. After suffering serious losses, the Vikings emerged as the winners and the Saxons were completely routed. Byrhtnoth was one of the Saxon casualties. After the Battle of Maldon, the Viking force that had disembarked on the eastern coast of England could have easily raided a large portion of the country without encountering serious resistance. Aethelred II, unlike his predecessors, was a weak monarch and did not have great military capabilities. In addition, the arrival of a new Viking army in England had spread panic among the population and thus it seemed that the resurgence of Danelaw was no longer impossible.

After the Battle of Maldon, the Archbishop of Canterbury, Sigeric, advised Aethelred II to pay off the Vikings instead of trying to defeat them. Sigeric was supported by most of the Saxon warlords of southeastern England and thus the king had no choice but to agree to their requests and come to terms with the foreign raiders. A danegeld tribute of 10,000 Roman pounds of silver (3,300kg) was paid to Olaf and his men, who left England.

The events of 991 showed the Vikings that the Saxon kingdom was too weak to repulse their attacks and that a new invasion of England was still possible. By simply appearing with their warships on the horizon, the Scandinavian warriors could terrorise the English population and force Saxon authorities to pay danegeld. Without fighting, the Vikings could obtain enormous sums of gold and silver that could have been plundered only after months of raids. The Scandinavians no longer had a stable presence in England, but they still represented a deadly menace.

Norwegian Vikings

During this phase, the Vikings from Norway started to play a prominent role as raiders, since the Danish 'first generation' pirates had changed their general strategy. An early form of centralised Danish kingdom was developing during those years and an increasing number of Danish Vikings – especially those from the southern regions of Jutland that bordered with Germany – were converting to the Christian faith.

In contrast, the Norwegian Vikings continued to live according to their traditional lifestyle and increased their raiding activities. During those years, Scandinavians who had settled in Normandy were gradually evolving into feudal warlords and knights. Since 911, in fact, the Vikings of Normandy had become vassals of the kingdom of France and their territories had been organised into the Duchy of Normandy. In practice, they were becoming Normans and gradually losing their original character of sea-borne raiders.

The 'feudalisation' of the Normans had some very important practical consequences for the Vikings. First of all, it led to the progressive disappearance of Scandinavian naval bases located in Normandy from which many raids directed against southern England had been launched. As a result, the new phase of

A housecarl of Cnut the Great, attacking with his two-handed Danish axe. (© Skjaldborg Vikings)

A Viking warrior equipped with corselet of scale armour. (© Compagnie de la Branche Rouge)

Viking incursions and invasions that was opening would have been characterised by a strong Norwegian character since the most important new bases were located in the fjords of Norway. The Viking force that fought at the Battle of Maldon was the last in which the warriors were mostly from Denmark. It should be noted, however, that after the establishment of the Danish kingdom, the Vikings from the latter realm continued to have some ambitious plans regarding England. Unlike the Norwegians, who were interested in raiding or in being paid with danegeld, the Danish Vikings were now starting to consider the possibility of a new permanent settlement in England. After being paid, Olaf Tryggvason was baptised a Christian, with Aethelred as his sponsor, and left the Saxon kingdom forever. Some of the warriors who had fought with him at Maldon, also decided to remain in England to serve as mercenaries and were garrisoned on the Isle of Wight.

Aethelred II, however, had not resolved his problems with the Vikings. In 997, his Scandinavian mercenaries revolted and left the Isle of Wight with the objective of raiding some of the nearby areas. Cornwall, Devon, Somerset and southern Wales were ravaged in 997; during the following year, the Vikings attacked Dorset, Hampshire and Sussex. In 999, the former mercenaries invaded Kent, before being paid with a second danegeld and leaving England for Normandy. During the following years, the Scandinavian raiders continued to attack the Saxon kingdom frequently because they had retained control over the Isle of Wight (which became their most important base). The weak Aethelred had no choice but to pay the Vikings with substantial amounts of gold/silver on many more occasions in order to save his kingdom and this caused great malcontent among his subjects. At that time there were still substantial Scandinavian communities living in England, on the former territories of the Danelaw. These were made up of peaceful individuals, who had been loyal subjects of the Saxon kings for decades.

Danish Vikings

The ethnic problems of the Saxon kingdom erupted in 1002, when Aethelred II ordered the massacre of all the Scandinavians living in his realm. In what became known as Saint Brice's Day Massacre, thousands of former Vikings were slaughtered by the Saxons. Among the many victims of the massacre ordered by the

Saxon monarch, was Gunhilde, sister of Sweyn Forkbeard, King of Denmark. In 1003, in retaliation that monarch launched a massive invasion of eastern England, with the objective of seeking revenge for the many Scandinavian civilians who had been slaughtered during the previous year and with the ambition of creating a new permanent settlement in the British Isles. The Danish Vikings raided East Anglia and sacked Norwich without meeting serious opposition. They later had to fight a pitched battle against a local warlord, from which they emerged victorious despite having suffered severe losses. In 1005, however, a very severe famine afflicted the British Isles and thus Sweyn Forkbeard's forces started to experience serious logistical problems. To avoid the risk of losing his entire invading army to starvation, the Viking monarch abandoned England after having obtained very little.

In 1009, a new Scandinavian invading force landed on the shores of the Saxon kingdom; this was commanded by the warlord Thorkell the Tall and comprised several thousands of warriors. Initially, the Vikings marched towards Canterbury, but they were paid by the local community with a large sum of money and thus did not invade the city. After this, they tried to take the City of London, but all attempts were repulsed due to the strong resistance of the Saxon military forces. In 1011, the Viking army returned to Canterbury and finally took it after a siege of three weeks; the same Archbishop of the city, Aelfheah, was taken as a hostage by the raiders. Thorkell continued to terrorise southern England with his men for several months, until he was paid several times by the local communities who offered him danegeld in order to save their lives and properties. In total, 48,000lb of silver was given to the Vikings before they left England during 1012.

Like other Scandinavian leaders before him, Thorkell decided to remain in the Saxon kingdom with some of his most trusted men in order

A Viking warrior wearing a thick tunic obtained from organic material. (© Vigamadr)

to serve as a mercenary for Aethelred II. In 1013, the Vikings of Denmark mounted a new large-scale invasion against England, which was led by Sweyn Forkbeard and by his son Cnut (the future Cnut the Great). The Scandinavian army landed at Sandwich and soon assumed control over most of East Anglia before moving to Northumbria. Here, there was still a significant presence of Scandinavians, who were unaffected by the massacre of 1002 and who welcomed the Danish warriors.

Sweyn and Cnut seemed unstoppable, especially because Aethelred was too slow in organising an effective military response. They conquered the five main cities of the former Danelaw, which were collectively known as the 'Five Boroughs': Derby, Leicester, Lincoln, Nottingham and Stamford. After coming over Watling Street, which was one of the most important land routes of Saxon England, the

Above left: A Viking warrior equipped with sword and round shield. Note the large dimensions of the brooch. (Photo Gunnar, © Dominika Černá)

Above right: A Viking warrior armed with two-handed axe and seax short sabre. (© Compagnie de la Branche Rouge)

Danish monarch advanced on Oxford and Winchester before moving against London. By now, it was clear that the Vikings wanted to assume control over the whole Saxon kingdom and thus the destiny of England was in their hands. Aethelred II and Thorkell reorganised their military forces and put up a strong resistance against the invaders around London. However, the Vikings prevailed, since only the areas of the Saxon capital had remained independent of their control. Aethelred understood that any further resistance would have been pointless and thus went to the Isle of Wight before leaving his kingdom in exile.

On Christmas Day 1013, Sweyn Forkbeard was proclaimed King of England: the Vikings had finally conquered the Saxon kingdom. A few weeks after these events, however, Sweyn died and a major revolt broke out among the Saxons (who had never accepted foreign rule). Upon the king's death, his older son Harald was proclaimed King of Denmark, while his younger son Cnut was declared King of England. Cnut, however, did not have chance to rule the realm, since Aethelred returned from exile and the whole Saxon population revolted against him. Cnut had to leave England to save his own life, and because Aethelred had formed a strong military alliance with the Norwegian warlord Olaf Haraldsson. The Saxon king reconquered his realm with the help of his new Norwegian allies, but when they too left England, he had to face a major revolt organised by his son and future successor Edmund Ironside. The beginning of a civil war in the Saxon kingdom offered a great opportunity to Cnut the Great, who soon organised his reconquest of England.

Chapter 3
Viking England

In the summer of 1015, while the civil war between Aethelred and Edmund was reaching its peak, Cnut landed on the English coastline at the head of a massive Viking army recruited from every corner of Scandinavia. According to modern reconstructions, Cnut the Great commanded a total of 10,000 warriors who were transported on 200 warships. This time the Vikings landed in Wessex, to menace the heart of the Saxon kingdom. The Scandinavians landed without meeting any serious opposition and thus raided several settlements. At that time, Wessex was still under control of Aethelred but he had been severely weakened by the rebellion of his son. When Eadric Streona, the Ealdorman of Mercia, changed side and joined the invaders, it became apparent that the old Saxon monarch could not continue his resistance for long. Also, Thorkell the Tall abandoned Aethelred and joined Cnut before the Vikings crossed the Thames and attacked Warwickshire. Edmund Ironside tried to stop the movements of the invaders on several occasions, but he was not able to achieve any significant result since the areas surrounding London were still loyal to his father. Understanding that the only way to slow down the enemy was to combine their forces, Aethelred and Edmund temporarily put aside their differences but achieved very little. Cnut occupied Northumbria and continued to enlarge the ranks of his troops by recruiting dissident Saxon aristocrats who were against the old king and his son.

On 23 April 1016, Aethelred died after many years of rule and was succeeded by his son Edmund; the latter was now the only supreme ruler of the Saxons, but this did not change the military situation in a significant way. The new monarch remained in London during the following months, since his troops were in no condition to conduct offensive operations. The Saxon capital was well defended with thick walls and had substantial food reserves; as a result, Edmund hoped that a long and victorious resistance could be possible. When the Scandinavians surrounded London, however, the Saxon king changed his mind and decided to go to Wessex in order to raise a new army there. Cnut the Great divided his army in two parts: one remained around London to block the city, the other went to Wessex with the objective of chasing Edmund. The siege of the Saxon capital was a difficult operation for the Vikings: they constructed dikes on the flanks of the city and dug a channel across the banks of the Thames in order to cut the communications upriver of the besieged. Meanwhile Edmund was able to raise a substantial military force in Wessex and fought two minor battles against the Scandinavian army that was on its tracks: the latter actions took place in Somerset and in Wiltshire, proving to be indecisive for both sides. In any case the Saxons were able to continue their march towards London and to relieve the city from enemy siege, after crossing the Thames at Brentford.

This victory, however, was very short-lived since Edmund soon had to march back to Wessex in order to replenish his losses. London was besieged again by Cnut, but also this time the city was not conquered by the Vikings.

This was the most delicate phase of the conflict, since both sides were by now exhausted. Eadric Streona decided to change sides and abandoned Cnut, who was ravaging Mercia in search of a decisive victory. In October 1016, the decisive battle for the destiny of England was fought at Assandon, in north-west Essex. Both Edmund and Cnut employed their best troops in the clash, the outcome of which was decided by Eadric Streona, who changed sides during the battle and gave victory to the Vikings of Cnut the Great. Edmund was soundly defeated and fled westwards, into Gloucestershire where he could count on the support of some Welsh nobles, but he was defeated again by the pursuing Vikings during a minor clash. After being wounded and having lost most of his supporters, the Saxon monarch had no choice but to accept the invaders. A peace treaty was signed between him and Cnut, according to which England would be divided in two parts. All the lands located north of the Thames would be ruled by Cnut, while all the lands located south of the Thames (including London) would be ruled by Edmund. Upon Edmund's death, Cnut would rule the whole territory of England. Just a few weeks after the signing of the treaty, Edmund Ironside died from the wounds suffered in battle and thus Cnut the Great could be crowned as the sole ruler of England.

In 1017, after decades of attempts and failures, the Vikings had finally completed their conquest of the English lands. Cnut ruled England for almost two decades and was one of the most brilliant kings in the history of the country. His rise to power stopped Scandinavian raids for a long period and thus an age of prosperity began for the Saxon population. In 1018,

A Viking warrior wearing a helmet with an aventail of chainmail on the back. (Photo Gunnar, © Dominika Černá)

after collecting a colossal 'danegeld' from his new kingdom, Cnut paid all his warriors and sent most of them home in order to preserve the internal stability of England. Only 40 Viking warships remained in England with their crews, which became a sort of standing army that was paid with a new special tax introduced by Cnut (and known as 'heregeld' or 'army payment'). The new king reorganised England from an administrative point of view, dividing the territory of his realm into four parts. Wessex remained under his personal control, Northumbria was assigned to Erik of Hlathir, East Anglia was given to Thorkell the Tall and Mercia remained in the hands of Eadric Streona. Over time, Cnut substituted his loyal Scandinavian followers with Saxon nobles he trusted and this helped him gain the support of most of the population.

Cnut the Great

While these events took place in England, the political situation in Scandinavia changed dramatically. Olaf Haraldsson, after returning to his homeland, had been able to free Norway from the influence of Denmark by winning the Battle of Nesjar in 1016, and thus had started to organise a first 'structured' Kingdom of Norway. During 1018, Cnut's brother and King of Denmark, Harald, died. This event, together with the ascendancy of Olaf Haraldsson, opened a new phase in Scandinavian history. After the sudden death of Harald II, Cnut the Great went to Denmark at the head of a fleet with the objective of claiming the Danish throne. After fighting a few minor clashes against some local opponents, he was crowned King of Denmark with the intention of returning to England in 1020.

An Anglo-Saxon noble wearing richly embroidered clothes. (© Skjaldborg Vikings)

A vast Viking empire was born in Northern Europe, which comprised England as well as Denmark. It was guided by the greatest warlord of the time, who still had expansionist ambitions. Cnut, in fact, had plans to dominate the whole Scandinavian world and thus would have attacked the Vikings of Norway and Sweden in the near future. By that time, those two countries were organised as two semi-centralised kingdoms: the first led by Olaf Haraldsson while the second was guided by Anund Jacob. These two kings feared that Cnut the Great could defeat them by using his superior military resources and thus decided to put aside their differences in order to form an alliance. Together they launched a series of attacks against Denmark and incited the local regent to revolt against Cnut.

During 1026, in order to restore his power in Scandinavia, Cnut assembled a large fleet of English/Danish warships and attacked the naval forces of his two enemies. A large battle was fought at Helgea, off the coast of Sweden, which saw the triumph of Cnut the Great. The Norwegian and Swedish Vikings were defeated in a decisive way, against all odds. In 1028, after travelling to Rome to receive the Pope's blessing and securing his position in England, Cnut the Great decided to bring Norway back under the influence of Denmark and sailed at the head of a fleet against Olaf Haraldsson. Olaf was not able to put up an effective resistance because the most important Norwegian warlords revolted against him so he had no choice but to surrender. As a result, Cnut added the Kingdom of Norway to his personal possessions. In 1030, Olaf Haraldsson tried to reconquer his former realm at the head of a Swedish army, but he was defeated and killed by the Norwegians at the Battle of Stiklestad.

Cnut the Great died in 1035 after having ruled a vast portion of Northern Europe for

Above left: A Viking spearman. Attached to the waistbelt there are both a seax and a knife. (Photo Skjaldborg Vikings, © Darling Muse Photography)

Above right: A Viking warrior armed with a one-handed axe, sword and knife. (Photo Gunnar, © Dominika Černá)

several years. In Denmark, he was succeeded by his son Harthacnut, who soon had to face a rebellion of the Norwegians. The Norwegians were able to restore the independence of their kingdom under the leadership of Magnus Haraldsson (son of Olaf Haraldsson). In England, instead, Cnut was succeeded by his other son Harold Harefoot. Harefoot was to rule the English lands on behalf of Harthacnut just while the latter was in Denmark, but in 1037 he decided to claim the English throne for himself and rebelled against his brother. The reign of Harold Harefoot continued until 1040, when Harthacnut was finally able to stabilise his position in Scandinavia and return to England with the objective of claiming his throne.

Chapter 4
Harald Hardrada

Denmark and England were ruled by Harthacnut until his death in 1042. After that year, both countries entered a very chaotic political phase. Control of Denmark was contested between a local pretender named Sweyn Estridsson and the Norwegian monarch Magnus Haraldsson. The hostilities came to a definitive end only in 1046, when Magnus died and Sweyn could remain as the sole ruler of Denmark.

In England, instead, the death of Harthacnut was followed by the re-emergence of the Saxon House of Wessex since Edward the Confessor, son of Aethelred II, was proclaimed king. He had spent most of his life as an exile in Normandy and thus, after his ascendancy to the throne, the Normans started to exert an increasing political influence over the English court. Edward the Confessor died without direct heirs on 5 January 1066, causing the beginning of the worst dynastical crisis ever in England during the central centuries of the Middle Ages. Four different pretenders, in fact, claimed their right to sit on the English throne. The first was Edgar Aetheling, who was just 15 in 1066 and the grandson of Edmund Ironside; the second was Harold Godwinson, Earl of Wessex, who was Edward the Confessor's brother-in-law but who had no blood connection with the defunct king; the third was Harald Hardrada, successor of Magnus Haraldsson and King of Norway since 1046, who had no blood ties with Edward the Confessor; the fourth was William, Duke of Normandy since 1035, who was a cousin of the defunct king through Edward's mother Emma (who was William's great-aunt). Edward the Confessor had promised his throne to both William and Harold during two different phases of his long life and this caused great confusion.

Edgar Aetheling
The weakest of the pretenders was Edgar Aetheling, who was the only one of the four who could not count on an army to support his claims.

Harald Hardrada
Harald Hardrada was a true Viking and had strong military forces, but his claims on the English throne were weak from a dynastic point of view; in 1064 he had already tried to become King of Denmark but his attempts had failed. He decided to invade England after concluding an important alliance with Tostig Godwinson, who revolted against his brother Harold

A common infantryman equipped with spear and round shield.
(© Skjaldborg Vikings)

A Viking settler armed with spear and seax. (© Compagnie de la Branche Rouge)

A Viking settler dressed in winter clothes. (Photo Skjaldborg Vikings, © Darling Muse Photography)

Godwinson after the latter was proclaimed King of England in 1066. From a political point of view, Harald Hardrada's landing on the English shores would have been perceived as just another Viking invasion by the local Saxon population. In any case the Norwegian warlord had good chances of victory, since in 1066 England would have been invaded simultaneously by two armies and thus Harold Godwinson would have been obliged to divide his military forces into two parts.

Harold Godwinson

Harold Godwinson, the Saxon leader, could count on the support of the most prominent nobles of his country, who were against the possibility of choosing a foreign king such as the Norman William or the Norwegian Harald. After Edward the Confessor's death, the Saxon nobles quickly elected Harold as their king in order to buy time in view of the upcoming military events. They knew that a Norman army and a Viking one would soon have attacked their country.

After hearing of Harold Godwinson's coronation, William of Normandy started assembling a massive fleet to transport his military forces to England. He could count on the support of the English church and of some nobles, who were against Harold's political plans. The new Saxon king prepared himself to face the Normans and recruited a very large army that comprised a significant number of professional warriors. The Saxons deployed themselves on the Isle of Wight and waited for the arrival of the Normans. The Normans, however, were blocked in their ports for seven months due to unfavourable weather conditions and thus William could not conduct his invasion with the planned timing. This delay caused significant problems to Harold too, since his plan was to defeat the Normans before facing a second invasion led by Norwegian Harald Hardrada. The Saxon king knew the Vikings would have needed some months to assemble a sizeable invasion force, unlike the Normans who could be ready to attack in a few weeks. The delay of seven months suffered by William meant that the two invasions would take place in the same time frame. Harold of Wessex knew that the Normans would have landed on southern England, but had no idea from which location the Vikings would attack; presumably, Harald Hardrada of Norway's target would have been East Anglia or Northumbria.

Harald Hadrada of Norway Attacks

The Vikings, travelling from Norway, landed on 8 September 1066, at the mouth of the River Tyne, and had Northumbria as their first target. As anticipated, their leader counted on the support of Tostig

Godwinson, who had revolted against his brother Harold and who had already tried to form an alliance with William of Normandy. When William refused his offer, Tostig went to the King of Norway and decided to join him in his invasion of England. The brother of the Saxon monarch proved to be a precious ally for Harald Hardrada, since he knew the terrain on which the Vikings were going to operate and also because he was in contact with several of the most important Saxon nobles of northern England. After joining his forces with those of Tostig, Harald sailed along the River Ouse towards the city of York. York had been the most important land base of the Vikings in England for a long time and its capture would be very important for the Scandinavian invasion force.

Harold Godwinson, the Saxon, had entrusted the defence of the northern part of his kingdom to the two most powerful warlords of the area: the Earl of Mercia, Edwin, and the Earl of Northumbria, Morcar, who were brothers. They had already mobilised part of their military forces in view of the Viking invasion and were able to move against Harald of Norway in order to prevent the fall of York. On 20 September, not far from the city, they fought at the Battle of Fulford. There were 10,000 Vikings in total, while the Saxons had assembled just 4,500 warriors (3,000 from Northumbria and 1,500 from Mercia). Edwin and Morcar, however, could deploy their forces in a good defensive position with the River Ouse on the right flank and a swampy area known as the Fordland on the left flank. Harald deployed his forces on higher ground, but was unable to form an encircling manoeuvre around the wings of his enemy.

At the beginning of the clash, the Saxons made a great mistake. Instead of remaining in their defensive positions, they launched a frontal attack against the Vikings. The Saxon offensive took place while the Scandinavians were still deploying their troops and was a complete failure. Harald organised a counter-attack with his best warriors and forced the Saxons to give ground. The decisive moment of the battle came when, against all odds, the Vikings were able to cross the River Ouse on one side and the Fordland on the other to attack the Saxons on three sides. Outnumbered and outmanoeuvred, the warriors of Edwin and Morcar fled from the battlefield. York was occupied by the Vikings soon after their victory and at that point it became clear that northern England was open to Harald Hardrada's conquest.

A Viking warrior armed with throwing axe.
(Photo Skjaldborg Vikings, © Darling Muse Photography)

Harold Godwinson Reacts

When news of the defeat at Fulford reached Harold Godwinson, the Saxon monarch was shocked but reacted rapidly. He forced his royal army to march 190 miles north from London to York to prevent raids in the northern part of his kingdom. Harold was a great military leader and within a week of the Battle of Fulford his forces were in situ facing Harald Hardrada around York. The Saxon warriors were extremely tired, since they had marched day and night for a week. However, they were more numerous than their opponents. According to modern estimates, the Vikings had lost 1,000 men at the Battle of Fulford and were now 9,000 in total. To oppose them, Harold had mustered 10,000 infantrymen and 2,000 cavalrymen. The Scandinavians were taken by surprise, not anticipating that the Saxon royal army could reach York in such a brief time.

The decisive clash of Harald Hardrada's invasion of England took place at Stamford Bridge, on the River Derwent. When the battle began, some of the Viking forces were on the west bank of the river while the majority were on the eastern bank since they had no idea that the Saxons were moving towards their positions. Caught by surprise, the Scandinavians on the east bank opted to deploy themselves into a defensive 'circle' formation. Those on the west bank were massacred and just a few were able to escape by crossing the bridge that gave the battle its name. At this point in the clash, Harold's troops had to pass across the bridge to attack the Vikings. According to contemporary sources, single-handedly a giant warrior from the army of Harald Hardrada (armed with a two-handed massive axe) blocked the narrow crossing and repulsed the Saxon warriors. He killed 40 of his enemies before a Saxon warrior floated under the bridge and thrust his spear through its planks to mortally wound the giant axeman. After pouring on to the eastern bank of the Derwent, the Saxons deployed a battle line just short of the Viking circle. Together they locked their shields and charged against the defensive formation of the enemy. The ensuing phase of the battle, characterised by harsh hand-to-hand fighting, lasted for hours and saw the Scandinavians resist with great determination. Both sides suffered heavy losses and the outcome of the clash was unpredictable.

Harald Hardrada fought with great courage among his elite warriors and tried to resist as long as possible. However, the defensive formation of the Viking army began to fragment and the initial cohesion was lost. The Saxons were able to break their enemy's 'wall

A Viking settler wearing a short-sleeved cuirass made of leather. (© Compagnie de la Branche Rouge)

of shields' and gradually surrounded isolated groups of Scandinavians. When it became clear that his army was in the process of being outflanked, Harald Hardrada did not attempt to abandon the battlefield but continued to fight at the head of his remaining warriors. He was killed by an enemy arrow before his troops went into a state of complete chaos. During this final phase of the clash, which saw the rout of the Viking army, Tostig Godwinson was also killed. When everything appeared lost for the Scandinavians, Viking reinforcements arrived on the battlefield. These warriors had been left behind by Harald to guard his warships and were under the command of his prospective son-in-law Eystein Orre. These Vikings launched a violent counter-attack against the Saxons, which was easily repulsed by Harold's men; and Eystein was killed during the fight. After several hours of intense combat, the Norwegian Harald Hardrada's impressive Viking army had been wiped out.

According to contemporary sources, so many Saxons and Norwegians died at the village of Stamford Bridge that the battlefield upon which the clash took place was still whitened with bleached bones 50 years after 1066. After obtaining such a brilliant victory, the Saxon Harold Godwinson concluded a truce with the surviving Vikings: they were allowed to leave England after giving pledges not to attack the Saxon kingdom again. Scandinavian losses were so severe that just 24 of their warships returned to Norway. Harold had destroyed the military force of one of his rivals, but the losses of his army had been substantial too.

Just three days after the Battle of Stamford Bridge, on 28 September 1066, William and his Normans landed in southern England on Pevensey Bay (Sussex). Without having the time to replenish his losses and to reorganise his troops, Harold had to march south rapidly at the head of his exhausted warriors. For the second time, the Saxon military forces had to cover an immense distance in a few days. When they arrived in the south to intercept the Normans, they were very tired but morale was extremely high.

A Viking settler armed with one-handed axe. (Photo Gunnar, © Dominika Černá)

Three weeks after Stamford Bridge, at the Battle of Hastings, the Saxons were defeated in a decisive way by the Normans and Harold Godwinson was killed by an enemy arrow. The glorious centuries of Saxon England finally came to an end and William the Conqueror could be crowned as the heir of Edward the Confessor. From a military point of view, the Battle of Stamford Bridge was a key factor behind the Norman victory of Hastings. It is sure, in fact, that if the Saxons had faced the Normans before fighting the Vikings, then the Normans would have had serious difficulties in breaking Harold's defences in southern England. The events of 1066 marked a turning point in the history of England but also for the Vikings. After being defeated at Stamford Bridge, the Scandinavians abandoned all plans to conquer the British Isles.

Chapter 5
William of Normandy

After crushing the Saxon royal army at Hastings, William hoped that the conquest of his new realm would be completed rapidly. The Saxon nobles and clergy, instead, chose not to surrender. Instead, they nominated Edgar Aetheling, son of Edmund Ironside, as their king and organised their resistance against the Norman invaders. William's first move was intelligent. He secured Dover, transforming it into his main naval base from which supplies and reinforcements could come from Normandy; then he secured the important religious centre of Canterbury. A token force was sent to occupy Winchester, where the Saxon royal treasury was preserved. In late November of 1066, he entered London, without facing any serious opposition. After crossing the Thames, William was in control of most of southern England. At that point, several of the Saxon aristocrats who had decided to resist after Hastings, including Edgar Aetheling, submitted to the Norman ruler without fighting. On Christmas Day, William was crowned King of England at Westminster Abbey. The new monarch, knowing that in northern England the local communities would resent his rule, tried to form a solid alliance with the Saxon nobles who had joined his cause by confirming their lands and titles. The religious hierarchy was also confirmed, since William was aware of the great power that the church held in England. Soon after assuming power, William returned to Normandy to stabilise his political position in northern France. One of his former local allies, Eustace of Boulogne, had begun a revolt against him.

While the Norman king was absent, the Saxons reorganised themselves in northern England under the guidance of Harold Godwinson's mother, Gytha. Gytha had power in the city of Exeter, where the Saxon resistance gathered a good portion of its military forces. In December 1067, William the Conqueror returned to England and besieged Exeter, which was conquered after a short siege. Meanwhile, other relatives of Harold, including his sons, landed near Bristol with the objective of launching a major revolt but were defeated by local Norman forces.

A Norman feudal knight armed with mace and sword.
(© Taillefer)

A Norman feudal knight armed with spear and sword. (© Taillefer)

In 1068, the Saxon warlords Edwin and Morcar, who had temporarily supported William after the Saxon defeat at Hastings, revolted against the Normans. The uprising of two of the most influential Saxon nobles represented a serious problem for King William. The only way for him to assume effective control over his entire realm was to defeat the Saxon aristocrats and replace them with loyal Norman nobles.

Feudalism, which was well established in Normandy, did not exist in England. An entire nobility, made up of landowners, was created. The Normans built a new network of castles across England, so that they could control their territory. Such fortifications would have been assigned to the new English nobles coming from Normandy and would have been defended by substantial garrisons.

The era that began following the uprising of Edwin and Morcar was characterised by a series of devastating military campaigns conducted in northern England. The Normans employed repressive methods to end all Saxon resistance. It was the so-called 'Harrying of the North', one of the most controversial pages in the personal history of William the Conqueror. In the summer of 1068, William invaded Northumbria and then occupied the city of York. Since the years of the Heptarchy, York had been the capital of the kingdom of Northumbria. Soon after taking York, the main Norman army left the urban centre but the garrison left behind was besieged by the Saxons. William was forced to return to Northumbria for a second time and to defeat the local rebels, while minor Saxon uprisings broke out practically in every corner of his realm.

Edgar Aetheling

By now Edgar Aetheling had changed sides and was at war with the Normans. The Saxon leader, however, knew that without help from abroad he would never have been able to defeat the invaders. Edgar made an alliance with Sweyn II, King of Denmark and a nephew of Cnut the Great.

Sweyn assembled a large fleet and sent it, at the orders of his sons, to the coast of Northumbria. The Danes raided the eastern coastline of England before conquering York and joined forces with the Saxon insurgents. The new menace was a particularly serious one, since the Scandinavian warriors who were now on English soil were professional fighters. In the winter of 1069, King William marched with his royal army from Nottingham to York, with the objective of fighting a pitched battle against his enemies; when he reached the city, however, the Danes had already moved with all their ships to the Humber Estuary. After these events, negotiations took place between William and the Danish leaders, with the king agreeing to pay a large sum to the Scandinavians in exchange for their promise of leaving England immediately and without fighting.

Once the Danish menace disappeared, William turned his attention to the Saxon rebels. He and his men acted in a very cruel way: many villages were burned to ashes, crops and herds were confiscated, hundreds of civilians were killed without a reason and the food reserves of the local communities were destroyed. These acts caused the death of more than 100,000 people, most of whom died of starvation. William was using psychological warfare to terrorise his enemies and to eradicate Saxon resistance in northern England.

The Norman acts of devastation were accompanied by the building of several new castles, most of which were, at least initially, only small fortifications made of wood. Castles were built in Warwick, Nottingham, York, Lincoln, Huntingdon, Cambridge, Chester and Stafford. By April 1070, William the Conqueror had pacified the northern part of his kingdom and could work to create a strong alliance with the English clergy. His conquest of the realm was officially recognised by the Pope, who sent three of his legates to Winchester to crown William in a new ceremony. In exchange for this religious investiture, the Norman monarch agreed to replace several Saxon bishops and abbots with French ones who could be controlled directly by the Pope.

King William, however, still had to face menaces from abroad affecting the stability of his kingdom. In the spring of 1070, in fact, Sweyn of Denmark attacked England again at the head of a large fleet. The Scandinavian monarch joined forces with local Saxon insurgents, but after weeks of campaigning he was able to achieve very little – except for looting some religious buildings – and thus returned home.

During 1071, William fought his main Saxon enemies again: Edwin and Morcar. This time, Edwin was betrayed by his own men and killed, while Morcar went to the Isle of Ely where he tried to resist. The Normans landed on the island, defeated and captured Morcar. In 1072, William faced a new foreign invasion, this time from the northern borders of his realm. King Malcolm of Scotland invaded northern England in the hope of gaining some border territories while the Normans were experiencing their own the internal troubles. William defeated Malcolm easily after a brief campaign and concluded a peace treaty with him. Edgar Aetheling, who had sought refuge in Malcolm's court, was expelled from Scotland as part of this treaty.

During 1073, King William had to leave England for Normandy, since his continental possession of Maine was attacked by the Count of Anjou. After a few weeks of fighting, the Norman monarch prevailed, but the general strategic situation of his French domains was worsening. The Count of Anjou

Duke William and his standard bearer discuss the impending battle. Both are equipped with an almond-shaped kite shield. (© Taillefer)

and the Count of Flanders were strongly determined to limit Norman power in northern France. To achieve their objectives, they could count on the decisive support of the King of France, who feared that William the Conqueror could become much more powerful than him.

England and France

In 1075, two Norman nobles who had received land properties in England, Ralph de Gael, the Earl of Norfolk and Roger de Breteuil, the Earl of Hereford, organised a plot with the objective of overthrowing William. Known as the 'Revolt of the Earls', this action was sponsored and supported by the King of France. William was absent when the rebellion began, but his loyal vassals were able to crush the revolt and quite rapidly. The insurgents had invited a Danish fleet of 200 warships to England, but it arrived too late.

Soon after these events, William had to face an invasion of his Norman domains by King Philip I of France. By 1076, King Philip was determined to reduce the territorial expansion and political power of the Duchy of Normandy. During this new war, William the Conqueror was defeated on the open field at the Battle of Dol. Despite this setback, however, the Normans went on to defeat enemy forces who later

A Norman saddle. The front and back pommels were specifically designed to provide more stability while riding and charging. (© Taillefer)

A Norman knight wearing a painted nasal helmet that is shaped like a Phrygian cap. (© Taillefer)

Duke William of Normandy equipped with nasal helmet and short-sleeved chainmail. The square on the chest was covered with chainmail on the external side and could be worn on the front of the face in order to protect it. (© Taillefer)

tried to invade Maine. During 1077, the hostilities between William and Philip temporarily came to an end, but at that point, the King of England started to experience troubles closer to home.

Robert, the eldest son of William, quarrelled with his younger brothers William and Henry in view of the succession to their father. Now that the ruling Duke of Normandy was also King of England, would his successor continue to control both territories or would they be divided? If so, would the eldest son receive Normandy or England? In 1078, Robert, who wanted the title to Normandy prior to the death of his father, rebelled against William. He was given decisive support by Philip of France, who assigned him the castle of Gerberoi on the border of Normandy. King William besieged his son and the rebels in Gerberoi. During the siege, a pitched battle took place between the opposing sides and in this clash William was unhorsed by Robert. The king was saved by one of his English soldiers but was defeated and had to abandon the siege of Gerberoi. In 1080, father and son found a compromise. The Duchy of Normandy was promised to Robert. He was more interested in becoming Duke of Normandy than receiving the English crown; Normandy, after all, was richer than England at that time and many Norman nobles still considered William's conquest of England as a 'temporary addition' to the Norman domains.

While King William was campaigning in Normandy against Robert, King Malcolm of Scotland invaded northern England and raided the area between the rivers Tweed and Tees. Encouraged by the foreign attack, the Northumbrians rebelled against the Normans. William responded by sending his son Robert to defend his land against the Scots, at the head of the royal army. Malcolm was defeated together with the Northumbrian rebels and the Normans built new fortifications to defend the border of northern England. During 1083, Robert rebelled again and renewed his alliance with the King of France. As a result, William returned to Normandy, where he had to fight in Maine to crush a local feudal revolt. The last years of William's long reign were troubled, since he had to fight the French monarch in Vexin. In July 1087, while burning the city of Mantes in Vexin, the English king suffered a fatal injury (probably caused by the pommel of his saddle). Before dying, William the Conqueror assigned the Duchy of Normandy to his first son Robert and gave the custody of the Kingdom of England to his second son William. Henry, his younger son, did not inherit any territories but received a large sum of money. Soon after the death of his father, William would be crowned King of England as William II.

Lasting Legacy

William the Conqueror was a capable military leader and an excellent administrator. He created a network of impressive fortifications in England made up of castles, keeps and mottes. The Tower of London was erected during his reign. William introduced feudalism in his new realm by assigning land properties to his most loyal nobles who – in turn – gave fiefdoms to the knights at their service (this was the so-called 'sub-infeudation' system). Each Norman earl was to provide a fixed quota of knights to the king for war service and to provide garrisons to the various castles in time of peace. William was well known for his love of hunting and introduced the so-called 'forest law' in several areas of England, according to which only authorised individuals could hunt on the territory of the royal forests. The Norman monarch never attempted to integrate Normandy and England into one unified political entity and thus – only for his French domains – he always remained a vassal of the French monarchy. William did not reform the Saxon administrative system based on shires; and as a result, royal authority continued to be represented in each by public officials called sheriffs.

The king spent most of his life travelling across his domains, in order to control his territories directly. Initially he had very little knowledge of his new subjects' economic capabilities and of his new realm's resources. William, however, continued the collection of the Saxon danegeld or land tax; an annual tax based on the value of landholdings. This could be collected at differing rates (usually two shillings per hide in standard years, rising to six shillings in years of crisis). William enlarged the royal territorial possessions in England by absorbing the lands previously owned by Harold Godwinson. This made

Detail of the helmet and chainmail worn by a Norman knight. (Photo Skjaldborg Vikings, © Ancient Armoury)

him the largest secular landowner of the kingdom by a wide margin. At Christmas 1085, William the Conqueror ordered the compilation of a survey of the landholdings held by himself and by his vassals throughout England. He also divided his realm into counties. The compilation resulted in the *Domesday Book*. This survey consisted of a listing made on a county basis that gave the holdings of each landholder grouped by owners. The document described each holding in great detail, providing its value and tax assessment as well as other information such as the number of peasants living on it, the number of ploughs that the locals had and the location of any significant natural or material resource. The *Domesday Book*, completed during 1086, is the most impressive record of feudal obligations ever produced during the Middle Ages. It is a perfect representation of William the Conqueror's administrative capabilities.

Chapter 6

The Vikings in the Celtic Nations

Wales

Due to its geographical position, Wales was not attacked by the Vikings with the same degree of violence that was experienced by England. During the early phase of the Scandinavian raids in the British Isles, the Vikings created some short-lived temporary settlements in Pembrokeshire and on the Gower Peninsula. The raiders, however, were not able to establish a significant presence due to the strong resistance of local aristocrats and to the lack of long rivers that could be employed by them as significant waterways. During the ninth century, Wales was strongly linked to the Celtic communities who lived in the French region of Brittany, which came under a strong Scandinavian influence in that period. After settling in Normandy, the Vikings established a solid alliance with the aristocrats of Brittany; this had positive consequences for the Welsh princes, who exchanged goods with the French Bretons and had strong cultural links with them. With the arrival of the Great Heathen Army and the ascendancy of Alfred the Great, however, relations between the Welsh and Vikings partly changed.

In 893, 250 Scandinavian warships appeared off the coast of the Lympne Estuary in Kent but no contingents were disembarked; after sailing along the coastline for some days, a large Viking military force disembarked and built a strong fortified position at Appledore. The invaders brought their wives and children with them, since they intended to create a permanent settlement. Alfred the Great did not attack the foreigners immediately, since he needed more time to gather his military resources. During the following weeks, the Vikings received significant reinforcements and resumed their advance from their base at Appledore. Alfred sent some of his troops, under the command of his son Edward, to stop the Scandinavians; a battle was fought between the two sides at Farnham (Surrey) a few weeks later, which ended with a victory for

A Viking settler equipped with a one-handed axe and round shield. (Photo Gunnar, © Dominika Černá)

A Viking settler armed with spear.
(© Compagnie de la Branche Rouge)

the Saxons. After these events the Vikings were defeated for a second time, again in Surrey, and so joined forces with another group of Scandinavians based at Shoebury in Essex.

The hostilities between the Vikings and the Saxons continued for several months, mostly because Alfred was preoccupied with other Scandinavian forces attacking other areas of England. Finally, the English monarch and his son were able to assemble a sizeable army in order to defeat the Vikings based in Essex once and for all. This military force comprised a significant number of Welsh warriors who had joined forces with those of the Saxons in order to eliminate a Scandinavian presence that represented a great potential menace to them too. The combined Saxon and Welsh military force attacked the Vikings and forced them to move north-west, where they were besieged at Buttington (Wales). The Vikings were blocked here for several weeks, and almost died of hunger. The few survivors surrendered, and the Saxons and the Welsh obtained a clear victory. After being defeated at Buttington, the Vikings no longer represented a menace for Wales and their raids in that area of the British Isles became very sporadic.

In 903, a group of Vikings travelling from Dublin occupied the island of Anglesey, with the objective of establishing a permanent foothold in Wales. This early attempt of colonising Anglesey failed but was followed by several Scandinavian raids against the island. Around 1000, a Viking stronghold was built there, but this fortified position was short-lived.

Cornwall, having much in common culturally with Wales, had occasionally been attacked by the Vikings since 833. During 1001–1003 the Scandinavians occupied the city of Exeter, but they were later expelled in a definitive way. The Viking presence in Wales was never significant, but the same cannot be said for Scotland and Ireland.

Scotland

The Viking presence in Scotland began with occasional raids launched against important religious sites, beginning in 794. The monastery of Iona, the most important in Scotland, was assaulted twice by the Scandinavians in 802 and 806. During the following decades, the Viking raids intensified, and large fleets of Scandinavian warships started to appear off the coasts of Scotland. As already discussed, the Scottish lands were divided into three main realms during the early ninth century: the large kingdom of Fortriu, the kingdom of Dál Riata and the kingdom of Strathclyde.

The first, populated by the warlike Picts, was the dominant military power of Scotland and was frequently at war with the other two kingdoms. Dál Riata was inhabited by the Scoti, who controlled the whole territory of Ireland, and thus had strong ties with that land; Strathclyde was populated by Britons who had a lot in common with the Welsh communities of the south.

In 839, a large Viking army landed in Scotland to conduct a massive incursion; to face this unexpected threat, the kingdom of Fortriu and the kingdom of Dál Riata formed an alliance and joined their military forces to defeat the Scandinavians. In what was the first major campaign fought in Scotland against the Vikings, the local warriors were utterly defeated in a bloody battle of which we know very little. The kings of Fortriu and Dál Riata were both killed during the clash. Over time, the Vikings conquered all the islands around Britain from the Isle of Man at the southernmost point to the Shetland Islands in the north; these new possessions formed an 'empire of the isles' and were used as important naval bases, especially to conduct raids against the Scottish coastline.

Moving from the Orkney Islands and the Shetland Islands, the Scandinavians attacked the northern areas of the Highlands, most notably Caithness and Sutherland. These locations were inhabited by the Picts of the Cat tribe, one of the most warlike communities of the kingdom of Fortriu, who enjoyed a certain degree of autonomy. Guided by experienced warlords such as Sigurd Eysteinsson and Thorstein the Red, the Vikings conquered Caithness and Sutherland before turning their attention to the southern

A Viking settler carrying spear and seax. (Photo Gunnar, © Dominika Černá)

areas of Ross and Moray (which were never conquered by them in a definitive way). The resistance of the local Picts was courageous but desperate, since they were quite isolated from the rest of the kingdom of Fortriu, while the Scandinavians could rely on the supplies coming from their bases in the northern islands.

The Viking territories of northern Scotland were unified in a single political entity, which gradually lost its original 'piratical nature' when the frequency of the Scandinavian incursions decreased. This area of the Highlands would continue to have a distinct Scandinavian character for the following two centuries, albeit as part of the kingdom of Scotland.

As we have seen, Orkney and Shetland were the main bases from which the Vikings attacked the northern portion of the Highlands. The western portion of the Highlands became the target of the Vikings coming from the Outer Hebrides and the Inner Hebrides. Unlike the events that determined the future of Caithness and Sutherland, however, the Scandinavians never established a permanent presence in the western Highlands since they conducted incursions only to capture slaves or to occupy coastal locations on a temporary basis.

A well-equipped Viking settler armed with spear, a one-handed axe and knife. Note the excellent manufacture of his fur cap. (Photo Gunnar, © Dominika Černá)

The Viking lands of northern Scotland were collectively known as Lothlend or Lochlainn and had been colonised since the beginning of the Scandinavian presence by Norwegian warriors. Initially these warriors were under direct control of the homeland, but gradually they created their own independent dynasty and started to be strongly linked with the Vikings of Ireland. The Scandinavian presence in the Highlands had important consequences for the political situation of Scotland, since it was an indirect but fundamental factor behind the unification of Fortriu and Dál Riata into a single realm.

Around 843, Kenneth MacAlpin became king of the Picts as well as of the Scoti from western Scotland. A new dynasty, known as the House of Alpin, was born and the first organised kingdom of Scotland (known as the kingdom of Alba since 900) started to emerge. After the unification of Fortriu and Dál Riata, the kingdom of Strathclyde became the main target of the Viking raids in Scotland. In 870, a large Scandinavian force coming from Ireland laid siege for four months to Alt Cnut in south-western Scotland; the campaign ended with victory for the Vikings, who captured the monarch of Strathclyde. Gradually the Britons of western Scotland lost their military capacity due to the frequent Scandinavian raids and so their kingdom became increasingly subordinate to the Saxon kingdom (kingdom of Alba).

In 937, the Saxons defeated the Britons of Strathclyde at the Battle of Brunanburh and installed a puppet king in western Scotland. Around 1030, when the Saxon kingdom experienced difficult times caused by Viking invasions, the kingdom of Alba took advantage of the ongoing situation to invade and annex the kingdom of Strathclyde. Despite being militarily strong, especially after their unification, the Picts and the Scots experienced great difficulties in containing Viking raids. After the Scandinavians established a permanent base in Dublin and occupied Northumbria, the new realm created by Kenneth MacAlpin was surrounded by hostile communities.

In 875, at the Battle of Dollar, the Picts/Scots were utterly defeated by a Viking army and suffered heavy casualties. After this clash, large portions of Scotland were raided by the Scandinavians, without serious opposition. Since 900, however, the general situation started to improve for the Picts/Scots after the more centralised and gaelicised kingdom of Alba gradually emerged. The new realm was the result of the fusion of the Picts and the Scots. The Picts represented the majority of the new kingdom's population, while the Scots extended their Gaelic culture to most of Scotland (the Picts were 'gaelicised').

A Viking settler with his dog. (Photo Gunnar, © Dominika Černá)

In 902, the Vikings lost their Dublin base and this helped the kingdom of Alba in exerting a stronger control over its western coastline. For Scotland, the 10th century was full of battles fought against the Scandinavians, and the kingdom of Alba emerged as the winner on several occasions. In 962, the Scots obtained a clear victory over the Vikings at the Battle of Bauds. After that clash, the Scandinavians ceased to represent a menace for mainland Scotland and continued to rule only the area of Lochlainn.

Following the ascendancy of the kingdom of Alba, the Scandinavians of Caithness and Sutherland were forced to deal with the Scots on almost equal terms. After having been autonomous for several decades, the Vikings of Lochlainn had returned under the influence of Norway by 1000 and were ruled by the Earldom of Orkney (a fiefdom of the Norwegians). In 1196, Harald Maddadsson, Earl of Orkney, agreed to become a fief of the kingdom of Alba and started to pay a monetary tribute for possession of Caithness and Sutherland to William I of Scotland. After this event, the Scandinavians living on mainland Scotland were gradually absorbed into the local population.

Ireland

The first recorded Viking raid in Irish history took place in 795, when a small group of Scandinavians, presumably from Norway, looted the small island of Lambay, not far from Dublin. Some years later, the pirates returned to conduct more devastating attacks in the same area as well as along the coastline of Connacht. Like those that took place in England and Scotland during this same period, these early raids shocked the local communities but did not cause major changes in the areas affected by them. The early Viking raiders, in fact, were searching for treasures to plunder and slaves to capture. The appearance of the Scandinavians marked the beginning of a new phase in the history of Ireland: the 'golden age' that had seen the Scoti/Gaels converting to the Christian faith came to an end and a new period characterised by violence and terror began.

Over time, the Vikings intensified their attacks against Ireland while focusing attention on the most important religious sites of the island. Just as in Scotland, they initiated their colonisation by conquering minor islands located around Ireland. As a result, the Skellig Islands soon became an important naval base. When the menace represented by the Vikings became significant, Ireland's nobles were unable to organise an effective response. At that time, the territory of Ireland was fragmented into several small kingdoms that were constantly at war with each other. Strong rivalry existed between the kingdom of Munster in the south-west and the kingdom of Leinster in the south-east. The Scandinavians used these internal divisions to their advantage and started planning a permanent settlement in Ireland.

From 820, the Vikings started to create fortified encampments, known as longports, along the Irish coastline. Here they spent the winter, when the weather did not permit raids. The fact that the Vikings preferred to remain in Ireland during winter instead of returning home indicates that they felt safe on Irish soil and that their Irish opposition was very weak. The most important of the longports was established on the River Liffey and was called Duiblinn; it would later become the largest Viking base in the British Isles and the first nucleus of present-day Dublin. After securing their positions on the coast, the Scandinavians began using the major rivers of Ireland to conduct long-range raids inland. These were particularly

A Viking archer. The Scandinavian longbow was effective if employed by a skilled warrior. (Photo Gunnar, © Dominika Černá)

A Viking archer. Note the practice of carrying the round shield on the back, in order to have additional protection and greater mobility. (Photo Gunnar, © Dominika Černá)

devastating and involved hundreds of warriors. Their usual targets were monastic settlements such as Armagh, Glendalough, Kildare, Slane, Clonard, Clonmacnoise and Lismore. The many victories obliged the Irish kings to rethink their politics, since unity was the only factor that could stop the Viking raids.

In 848, the kingdom of Munster and the kingdom of Leinster joined military forces to face a large Scandinavian army that had landed in Ireland. The Irish warriors achieved a significant victory over the Vikings, but it only stopped Viking incursions for a short time. After 848, the Scandinavians adopted a new strategy: instead of fighting against all the kingdoms of Ireland at the same time, they formed local alliances with some of them and offered their services as mercenaries to the nobles who were involved in Irish internal conflicts.

Two Viking warlords, named Olaf and Ivar, were particularly active in Ireland during this period. They concluded alliances with several Irish kings and changed sides according to circumstances. With superior military capabilities, the Scandinavians could determine the outcome of a local conflict and were particularly appreciated as mercenaries by the Irish warlords of the time. Occasionally, Irish warlords were able to annex other kingdoms to their realms and thus assumed the title of High King. This was little more than an honorific title, since every attempt at political unification usually ended with failure. While the Irish aristocrats killed each other in futile and interminable wars, the Vikings operating from Dublin could take advantage.

Generally, the opposition to the Scandinavians was stronger in northern Ireland since the southern part of the island was exhausted by the frequent clashes fought between Munster and Leinster. Around 873, however, the Vikings of Ireland experienced a period of crisis when both Olaf and Ivar died; an internal conflict broke out to determine the identity of their successors and this had negative consequences for the system of longports. The Irish rulers took advantage of the temporary Scandinavian weakness to organise a joint attack against the Viking base of Dublin. The Norwegians lost Dublin in 902, a year that brought serious military difficulties. For a few years, the Vikings were expelled from Ireland, but in 914 two new fleets from Norway appeared along the Irish coast. The first, guided by Ragnall, disembarked its warriors at Waterford, while the second, commanded by Sitric, stopped near Leixlip. The Irish assembled two armies to stop the Vikings: one attacked Ragnall in Munster, but was unable to engage the Scandinavians in a decisive battle. The other moved against Sitric in Leinster and was utterly defeated at the Battle of Confey. Following their victories, the Vikings resumed their march and reconquered Dublin.

In 918, Ragnall left Ireland and went to England in order to assume control over the Viking territories in Northumbria; as a result of this move, the Norwegian raiders could start exerting their influence over a large portion of the British Isles that lay between Dublin in the west and York in the east. Between 914 and 922, the Vikings created a series of permanent settlements

A Norman feudal knight. The spear is designed to be used during frontal charges. (© Skjaldborg Vikings)

in southern Ireland in Waterford, Cork, Wexford and Limerick to secure their grip on the island. Gradually the Scandinavians living in these centres started to mix with the local Irish population, initiating a period of co-existence based on intermarriage. A new mixed culture emerged, that of the Norse-Gaels; these had a solid presence in southern Ireland and were quite strong militarily. However, they were always considered as potentially hostile 'half-foreigners' by the Irish communities who lived in the centre and in the north of the island.

In 919, a large military coalition, comprising most of the Irish kingdoms, sent an army against the Vikings of Sitric with the objective of expelling them. As in 902, the most important target of the Irish military forces was represented by Dublin. A decisive battle was fought between the two sides at Islandbridge, which ended with a great Scandinavian victory: hundreds of Irishmen were killed, together with six of their kings who had participated in the clash. After the Battle of Islandbridge, the Irish military coalition was broken and the Vikings could continue their expansion across the island. In 920, Ragnall died and Sitric replaced him as the leader of Scandinavian Northumbria; as a result, a new leader named Gofraid emerged among the Vikings of Ireland.

Gofraid launched a series of offensive campaigns in Ulster, with the objective of

A Norman feudal knight wearing nasal helmet. (Guljara Photography, © Stronghold Re-enactment)

conquering the entire eastern half of Ireland. During 921–927, however, the Vikings were unable to achieve any significant result due to strong Irish opposition. In this historical phase, the Irish resistance was guided by Muirchertach mac Néill, a capable warlord who had great military skills. In 927, Sitric died and Gofraid went to York to replace him as the leader of Northumbria. Once in England, however, Gofraid was defeated by another pretender and thus was forced to return to Dublin without having achieved his objective. During his absence, a civil war had erupted between the Vikings of Ireland. The Scandinavians from Limerick had attacked those based in Dublin and occupied that settlement. Upon his return, Gofraid was able to reconquer Dublin but not to crush the rebels of Limerick. The conflict between Dublin and Limerick continued after Gofraid's death (934) and ended only in 937 when the Vikings of Ireland unified under the leadership of Gofraid's heir. In that year, the Irish Vikings formed a strong military alliance with the kingdom of Alba and the kingdom of Strathclyde against the Saxons of England, with the intention of increasing their influence over the British Isles. The large anti-Saxon

Above left: A Norman feudal knight equipped with short-sleeved hauberk of chainmail. (Guljara Photography, © Stronghold Re-enactment)

Above right: A Norman feudal knight wearing a decorated version of a nasal helmet. (© Skjaldborg Vikings)

alliance organised by Dublin, however, was defeated decisively at the Battle of Brunanburh (costing the kingdom of Strathclyde its independence).

In 944, during a new age of internal conflicts for the Scandinavians of Ireland, an Irish army was able to attack and sack Dublin but this was a short-lived victory since a Viking counter-offensive soon followed. During the period 950–980, the Vikings of Ireland formed a series of temporary alliances with various Irish rulers, taking part in several conflicts that ravaged the island but only to pursue their own interests. By that time, in fact, the Scandinavian settlement centred on Dublin was quite large and organised as a proper 'kingdom'. In 980, however, the Vikings were utterly defeated at the Battle of Tara, which was fought against an alliance of Irish rulers who wanted to eliminate the Scandinavian presence in southern Ireland. According to contemporary sources, the Battle of Tara was a massacre for the Vikings, who suffered heavy casualties. After the clash, the Irish forces besieged Dublin and obliged the Vikings to surrender a large number of slaves and valuables in exchange for their lives. The Battle of Tara was a turning point in the long history of the Irish Vikings, since it marked the beginning of their decline.

After the clash, the King of Dublin had to submit to the High King of Ireland. During the last decades of the 10th century a new prominent military leader emerged among the Irish aristocrats: Brian Boru, King of Munster since 978 and one of the greatest historical figures of the Irish Middle Ages. In 977, even before becoming ruler of Munster, Brian obtained an important victory over the Vikings of Limerick and annexed their territory to his possessions. One of the key elements of his policy was the ambition to expel all Scandinavians from Ireland. The warlord had a precise political vision: he wanted to become High King of Ireland by uniting all the realms of the island against the foreigners in a single 'national' effort. Initially, Brian Boru spent most of his energy conducting minor wars against other Irish monarchs, since he needed to impose his will over the various areas of southern Ireland before opening hostilities with the Vikings. By that time the Norse-Gaels had lost most of their unity, since each Viking settlement in Ireland pursued its own interests. For example, there was a strong rivalry between Limerick and Waterford that Brian Boru exploited to his advantage. He concluded a temporary alliance with the Vikings of Waterford before conquering Limerick.

A Norman feudal knight. Note the presence of some proto-heraldic symbols on the pennon of the spear and on the external surface of the shield. (© Skjaldborg Vikings)

The Scandinavians were well integrated into the Irish political system and their settlements acted exactly like the small Irish realms, but their presence was still perceived as a potential menace by most of the Irish population. Since 982, Munster and Leinster had fought each other in a series of violent conflicts, ultimately to determine the ascendancy of one kingdom or the other. Militarily, due to the continuous wars fought against the Vikings, Munster and Leinster were the strongest realms of Ireland with roughly equivalent resources. As a result, the role played by the Norse-Gaels was going to be decisive in order to determine the victory of one kingdom or the other.

In 997, after suffering several setbacks, the monarch of Leinster was forced to submit to Brian Boru and recognised his supremacy over southern Ireland. In 999, Brian had to face a military coalition organised against him and which comprised the kingdom of Leinster and the kingdom of Dublin. The first had not yet fully accepted Munster's dominance over southern Ireland, while the Scandinavians of the second were willing to regain their previous autonomy by freeing themselves from Irish political influence. The Irishmen of Leinster and the Norse-Gaels of Dublin assembled a large military force, which comprised a substantial number of Vikings. Brian Boru faced them at the head of an army that deployed warriors from Munster as well as from the kingdom of Meath. At that time, the monarchs of Meath had the honorific title of 'High Kings of Ireland' but their power was gradually declining in favour of Brian Boru's kingdom of Munster.

A Norman feudal knight, attacking with his sword. (Guljara Photography, © Stronghold Re-enactment)

On 30 December 999, the warriors of Munster/Meath met their enemies from Leinster and Dublin at the Battle of Glenmama. The clash took place in a narrow valley that had been a Leinster stronghold for centuries. According to ancient sources, it was a massacre, since the warriors of both sides fought with incredible determination. The Vikings of Dublin lost around 7,000 men. The Battle of Glenmama was a triumph for Brian Boru: he captured the ruler of Leinster and continued his advance towards Dublin. Since 980, and until revolting in 999, Dublin had been under the influence of the kingdom of Meath, but the ascendancy of Brian was to change all this. He entered Dublin without meeting any serious opposition and burned the settlement, plundering and killing with great violence. After these events, the kingdom of Dublin submitted to Munster and started to provide military contingents to Brian Boru, who then turned against his allies from the kingdom of Meath with the ambition of becoming the new High King of Ireland.

By 1002, after two years of war, the ruler of Meath submitted to Brian, who could now assume his long-desired honorific title. A single monarch now controlled, directly or indirectly, four of the most important Irish kingdoms: Munster, Leinster, Dublin and Meath. During the period 1002–11, Brian Boru conducted a series of campaigns in northern Ireland, with the objective of submitting the kingdom of Uí Néill and the kingdom of Ulaid. Ulaid had not been affected by the Viking incursions in a significant way and had never been dominated by any realm from southern Ireland. By 1011, despite experiencing several difficulties, Brian Boru was able to obtain the submission of every single Irish monarch and thus was the first king in the history of the island who could exert his political influence over the south as well as over the north.

In 1012, however, a major revolt broke out against Brian Boru, which saw the participation of Munster's worst enemies: the kingdoms of Uí Néill, Leinster and Dublin. These formed a strong military coalition in the hope of breaking Munster's predominance over Ireland. The allied kings knew that Brian was militarily much stronger than them and sought warriors from outside Ireland. Sigtrygg Silkbeard, the King of Dublin, was sent to the Orkney Islands and to the Isle of Man to raise large numbers of Viking mercenaries. By promising the crown of Ireland to the Scandinavians, he obtained the support of Sigurd Hlodvirsson (Earl of Orkney) and of Brodir of Man.

While Brian Boru camped outside the city of Dublin with his military forces, thousands of Scandinavian warriors came to Ireland in order to support his enemies. It should be remembered that in those same months, the Danish Vikings were conquering the kingdom of England and the possibility of Ireland becoming part of the Scandinavian domains was not so remote. The Viking fleets from the Orkney Islands and Isle of Man reached the port of Dublin during the holy week of 1014.

With the arrival of the Scandinavians, the anti-Munster coalition could deploy 7,000 warriors, matching Brian Boru. As a result, the outcome of the upcoming clash would be decided by valour and the

A Norman feudal knight. Note the excellent manufacture of his sword. (Guljara Photography, © Stronghold Re-enactment)

skills of the single military commanders. The ensuing Battle of Clontarf was fought just north of the Dublin settlement, between two armies that were similarly equipped. Brian Boru's enemies deployed themselves in three lines: in the first were the Scandinavian newcomers; in the second were the Norse-Gaels from the kingdom of Dublin; and in the third were the Irishmen from the kingdom of Leinster. According to ancient sources, Brian deployed allied Irish Vikings among his warriors coming from Munster.

The clash between the two armies reached an impressive level of violence, since neither side could have any chance of survival if defeated. Brian Boru's son, in particular, fought with enormous courage against the Scandinavian newcomers and killed many. The Vikings from the Orkney Islands and the Isle

A Norman feudal knight equipped with sword and kite shield. (Guljara Photography, © Stronghold Re-enactment)

of Man were all equipped with chainmail, while the warriors from Munster mostly fought as light skirmishers armed with throwing javelins. Thanks to their superior mobility, the Irishmen ensured severe losses to their opponents. The Battle of Clontarf lasted all day, since neither side was strong enough to gain the upper hand. At a certain point, however, the lines of the warriors from Dublin and Leinster broke. The Scandinavians fell back in search of safety. The ensuing retreat of the Vikings became a massacre, since they were slowed by the crossing of the River Tolka during their retreat towards Dublin. When the Scandinavians reached their warships, they learned that the tide had already come in and that their vessels had been carried away.

At this point, being desperate, they had no choice but to fight on the beach to the last man. Many Vikings were drowned during this final phase of the clash, but their leaders continued to fight with enormous courage. Murchard, the son and heir of Brian Boru, killed the Earl of Orkney, Sigurd, but shortly afterwards he himself was killed. Brodir of Man killed Brian Boru but in turn he was killed by Boru's brother, Ulf the Quarrelsome. The Battle of Clontarf, a great victory for Munster, marked the end of the Viking Age in Ireland but also the beginning of a great political crisis caused by the sudden death of Brian Boru and of his direct heir. The high degree of political unity that had been reached in Ireland under Brian was completely lost and a new season of internecine conflicts started. In 1052, the kingdom of Dublin was annexed by the kingdom of Leinster, thus bringing to an end the Scandinavian presence in the future Irish capital. With the Irish conquest of Limerick in 977 and of Dublin in 1052, the smaller Viking settlements in Ireland continued to exist for some time, but were rapidly transformed into minor political entities that were absorbed into the major Irish kingdoms.

During their incursions against mainland Britain and Ireland, the Vikings frequently operated from naval bases located on the minor islands surrounding the British Isles. It was part of their strategy, in fact, to establish some logistic centres not far from their targets. Since the Saxons, the Picts and the Scoti all had limited naval capabilities in comparison, the Scandinavians could easily create an empire of the isles around mainland Britain by conquering all the minor islands of the region. The Vikings divided the islands into two major groups: the Northern Islands and the Southern Islands. The first comprised the

Shetlands and the Orkneys, which remained under a strong Norwegian influence for most of the Middle Ages; the second comprised the Hebrides, the Isle of Man and the Islands of the Firth of Clyde. The Southern Islands were progressively assembled into a Scandinavian insular realm, known as Kingdom of the Isles, which existed as an independent political entity until the second half of the 13th century.

Shetland Islands

Located at the extreme north of the British Isles, the Shetlands were inhabited by sparse communities of Picts before the arrival of the first Viking pirates. Due to their relative proximity to Norway, they soon became the target of frequent Scandinavian incursions. During the last decades of the 8th century, while the Viking attacks against Britain and Scotland were still sporadic, the Shetlands were rapidly colonised by the Scandinavians, who transformed them into a base for their sea-faring raids. In 875, they were officially annexed to Norway and were united with the Orkney Islands in order to form an earldom that was assigned to the important Viking warlord Rognvald Eysteinsson.

During the last decades of the 10th century, the inhabitants of the Shetland Islands converted to Christianity. By that time, the Earls of Orkney, who ruled the Shetlands, exerted their control over the Viking footholds in the Highlands (Caithness and Sutherland). Since 1196, in order to retain possession of their lands on the Scottish mainland, the Earls of Orkney became fiefs of the kingdom of Alba while remaining fiefs of the kingdom of Norway. Apparently, however, the Shetlands remained under sole Norwegian influence, unlike the Orkneys. During the first half of the 13th century, the Scottish influence over the Orkneys and the Shetlands became increasingly strong. From 1231, for example, the earls who controlled the islands were all nobles from the Scottish mainland and not from Scandinavia. In 1263, war broke out between the kingdom of Scotland and the kingdom of Norway, since the monarch of Norway wanted to expand his possessions from the Orkneys to the Highlands. The conflict did not last long and resulted in failure for the Norwegians. The ensuing Treaty of Perth, signed in 1266 between Scotland and Norway, confirmed Norwegian suzerainty over the Orkneys and Shetlands. The Shetlands were officially ceded by the kingdom of Norway to Scotland only in 1471.

Orkney Islands

Before the arrival of the Vikings, the Orkneys were part of the Pictish kingdom of Fortriu. The first Scandinavian incursions against the islands took place during the last decades of the 8th century and were soon followed by an age of progressive colonisation. The Orkneys, in fact, became the main headquarters of the Viking warships operating against Scotland. Since 875, the Orkney Islands had been under Norwegian control and were united with the Shetlands in order to form an autonomous earldom. After converting to Christianity during the last years of the 10th century, the inhabitants of the Orkneys gradually came under the joint influence of Norway and Scotland, since their earls had some possessions in the Highlands. From 1231, both the Orkneys and the Shetlands were ruled by aristocrats who came from mainland Scotland and not from Norway. In 1471, the Orkney Islands were annexed to the kingdom of Scotland, like the Shetland Islands.

Hebrides

Prior to the early Scandinavian incursions, the Inner Hebrides were part of the kingdom of Dál Riata and inhabited by Scoti, while the Outer Hebrides were part of the kingdom of Fortriu and populated by Picts. Due to their strategic position, the Hebrides were raided several times during the early decades of the 9th century and soon became an important base for Scandinavian pirates. Around 885, they came under direct Norwegian control but this did not last for long, since the people revolted against Harald Fairhair of Norway. The Norwegian warlord sent one of his best men, Ketill Flatnose, to the Hebrides,

A Norman feudal knight armed with axe. (Guljara Photography, © Stronghold Re-enactment)

with orders to crush the rebellion. Ketill, however, occupied the Hebrides for himself and started to rule them as an independent monarch. This event marked the birth of the Kingdom of the Isles, a Viking realm centred on the Hebrides.

In 990, Sigurd the Stout, Earl of Orkney, took control of the Hebrides, but this political change did not last for long, since the kingdom of the Isles regained its independence in 1014. The following years saw the Vikings of Dublin starting to exert a solid influence over the Hebrides as well as over the Isle of Man (which came under direct control of the kingdom of Dublin for some time). In 1079, the Isle of Man became part of the Kingdom of the Isles, after having been an autonomous Scandinavian possession for several decades. Some years later, in 1098, the Norwegians sent a fleet to retake control of the Kingdom of the Isles. This attempt failed and the Hebrides continued to be ruled as an autonomous Scandinavian realm. The 12th century was characterised by a series of internal conflicts, which were complicated by the external influences exerted by Norway and Scotland. These 'civil wars' saw the temporary separation of the Inner Hebrides from the kingdom of the Isles and a series of naval battles. The kingdom survived as an independent state after this turbulent era, albeit with a less 'piratical' nature.

Since 1164, the reunified realm started to be ruled by Norse-Gael nobles coming from Scotland, who became known as 'lords of the Isles' and who had strong links with the Scottish mainland. These aristocrats were fiefs of Norway as 'kings of the Isles' but also fiefs of Scotland, since they held rich possessions on the Scottish mainland. In 1249, a large Scottish fleet, commanded by Alexander II, tried to occupy the Kingdom of the Isles but failed completely; this event led to the Norwegian expedition of 1263 against Scotland and finally to the signing of the Treaty of Perth in 1266. The latter gave the Hebrides and the Isle of Man to the kingdom of Scotland and thus put an end to the long history of the Kingdom of the Isles.

Isle of Man

Located between Ireland and Scotland and thus between the Viking centres of Dublin and York, the Isle of Man always had a great strategic importance for the Vikings. During the period 800–815, the island was plundered several times by the Scandinavians, who were initially interested only in raiding and in capturing slaves. By 880, however, the first permanent Scandinavian settlements had already been established on the Isle of Man. During 990–1079, it came under the direct rule of the kingdom of Dublin, which was greatly interested in the naval potential of the island. In 1079, the Isle of Man was absorbed into the Kingdom of the Isles. When that entity ceased to be an independent realm, the Isle of Man was absorbed into the kingdom of Scotland according to the Treaty of Perth (1266).

Firth of Clyde

The mouth of the River Clyde and its nearby islands were the heart of the kingdom of Dál Riata before the arrival of the Vikings. The early Scandinavian raids in the region were quite destructive and lasted for several decades, until a new age of permanent settlement by the Vikings began. Despite being quite small and having little population, the islands of the Clyde became an important Scandinavian naval base and thus were absorbed into the Kingdom of the Isles. For some periods, Vikings settled on small islands exerted their control also over the mouth of the River Clyde; in any case, the Firth of Clyde marked the boundary between the kingdom of Scotland and the Kingdom of the Isles until 1266.

Chapter 7

The Birth of Normandy

France, together with England, was one of the main targets of the Scandinavian raids during the two centuries of the Viking Age. Normandy, in particular, was greatly exposed to the attacks of the Scandinavians due to its geographical position; being a peninsula stretching from northern France towards southern England, it was a perfect location for the Viking naval bases. Its actual name derives from 'Northmannia', a term that can be translated as 'land of the Norsemen'. When the Scandinavian incursions in France began, that country was still part of the mighty Carolingian Empire that had been created by Charlemagne. At the height of its power, the Frankish Empire dominated most of continental Europe: from Catalonia in northern Spain to the lands of the Frisians in the Netherlands, from Brittany in north-western France to the heart of Germany.

Charlemagne, one of the greatest military leaders of the Middle Ages, died in the early days of 814. He had transformed Europe during his long reign, uniting most of the Germanic kingdoms that had emerged from the collapse of the Roman Empire into a single political entity. The great monarch was succeeded by his son Louis the Pious, who was able to preserve the unity of the Carolingian Empire despite the emergence of the Vikings and the outbreak of some bloody civil wars inside the Frankish world.

When Louis the Pious died in 840, a new civil conflict broke out between his three sons: each wanted to become emperor. The hostilities finally came to an end in summer 843, when the extremely important Treaty of Verdun was signed between the three pretenders to the Carolingian throne. According to its terms, the vast Frankish Empire was divided into three new states: West Francia, Middle Francia and East Francia. West Francia, roughly corresponding to present-day France, was given to Charles the Bald; Middle Francia, comprising the Rhineland and northern Italy, was assigned to Lothair I, who also inherited the imperial title, and East Francia, comprising most of western Germany, became the reign of Louis the German. The three new states had different destinies: West Francia gradually became the kingdom of France while East Francia became the Holy Roman Empire. The lands of Middle Francia ceased to be autonomous in 870 when the Treaty of Meerssen partitioned them between Charles the Bald and Louis the German. Due to the frequent civil wars and many territorial changes, during the period 840–870 the territories

A Norman feudal knight armed with sword. (Guljara Photography, © Stronghold Re-enactment)

of the former Carolingian Empire became extremely weak militarily; this assisted the Vikings, who could attack the isolated Frankish communities without having to face large armies.

As anticipated above, most of the Scandinavian raids conducted on mainland Europe had as their target the emerging kingdom of France or West Francia. Some early Viking incursions in France took place during the very last years of Charlemagne's reign, but it was under Charles the Bald that they became a significant problem for the French monarchy. The first recorded Scandinavian attack in France took place during 799 and was soon followed by a few others. In response to these early raids, around 810, Charlemagne organised a form of coastal defence in the northern regions of his empire but this was never fully implemented. In 820, during the reign of his son Louis the Pious, a major Scandinavian incursion was repulsed at the mouth of the River Seine. In 834, the Vikings launched a new attack against Frisia, on the territory of the present-day Netherlands, and were successful. The following years saw an escalation of raids: Antwerp, Rouen and Nantes were all attacked by the Scandinavians who were exploiting the weakness of the Frankish military system. In March

A Norman heavy infantryman wearing metal greaves.
(Photo Skjaldborg Vikings, © Darling Muse Photography)

845, a large fleet of Danish Vikings, with 120 warships, entered the Seine under command of Ragnar Lodbrok. The target of the Scandinavian raiders was Paris, one of the richest cities of West Francia (capital of that kingdom since 987). Charles the Bald was determined to fight to the death to defend the city and soon mobilised his military forces, dividing them in two: one half was deployed on the eastern bank of the Seine, the other on the western bank. At that time, Paris was still relatively small and did not extend beyond the Ile de la Cité, a natural river island located in the middle of the Seine.

After defeating one of the two Frankish armies and killing all the captured enemies in order to spread terror, Ragnar and his men landed on the Ile de la Cité on Easter Sunday. The Scandinavians plundered

A Norman heavy infantryman armed as a spearman. (Guljara Photography, © Stronghold Re-enactment)

Paris with great violence, killing many civilians. After some days, having obtained everything they wanted, they left the French city, but also because a plague had broken out inside their camp (at that time the banks of the Seine were covered by marshes, an inhospitable natural environment). Before returning home, however, the Scandinavians obliged Charles the Bald to pay them an immense sum of money: 7,000lb of French gold and silver. This was the first danegeld paid by the Frankish monarchs to the Vikings, which was followed by several others.

In the 840s, the Scandinavians attacked and pillaged several locations in Normandy, such as Rouen, with a predilection for the richest religious sites. Due to the presence of many navigable rivers, the Vikings could easily move across northern and central France. The Franks were completely surprised by their ability to sail upriver and could do very little to counter the enemy attacks. By penetrating deeply into the heart of France, the Scandinavians realised it could easily become a 'land of conquest' for them. With time, the Vikings started to attack the interior areas of the western Franks with more frequency and with larger numbers of warships. The Frankish military system, based on elite field armies that were too large to be moved rapidly, lacked the needed flexibility to create highly mobile 'task forces' that could counter the Scandinavian raids taking place along the rivers.

In 864, Charles the Bald tried to resolve this problem by issuing the so-called Edict of Pistres, which contained a series of practical measures that were aimed at protecting French cities and rural areas from Viking attack. With the new edict, the Frankish monarch created a large force of cavalry that had to serve on a permanent basis as an anti-raider 'special corps'. All French subjects who were able bodied and who owned a horse had to enlist in the new cavalry force and could be called to serve with very short notice by the royal authorities. The high mobility of cavalry would have countered the rapidity of the Scandinavian raids and would have enabled the French to attack the foreigners before they could re-embark on their warships to leave France.

The Edict of Pistres contained other important measures, such as the order to build fortified bridges at all the towns located on rivers; these would prevent the Vikings from sailing into the interior areas of France as well as transporting large booties on their ships after their incursions.

Unluckily for the French, however, most of the local communities did not have the needed resources to build new fortified bridges and only a few were effectively constructed. The edict promulgated by Charles the Bald also prohibited all trade in weapons with the Scandinavians. Selling horses to the Vikings was forbidden and any infraction to the new measures was punished with death. Charles the Bald's main

Above left: A Norman heavy infantryman, carrying his kite shield on the back. (Guljara Photography, © Stronghold Re-enactment)

Above right: A Norman heavy infantryman equipped with simple conical helmet and short-sleeved chainmail. (Guljara Photography, © Stronghold Re-enactment)

objective, in fact, was preventing the Scandinavians from establishing permanent bases in his realm. Following the Edict of Pistres, many French nobles started to build castles and fortifications on their territories in order to defend their peasant communities from the constant threat of Viking invasion. The building of private castles did nothing but reduce the power of central government and the control it had over the many nobles in the kingdom of France (who became increasingly autonomous, ruling as local monarchs).

During their incursions against Normandy, the Scandinavians understood that the nearby region of Brittany resented Frankish rule, and so they concluded an important military alliance with the Bretons. Of Celtic descent, the Bretons had been subjugated by the Franks during the reign of Charlemagne. They had stronger cultural links with the Britons of Wales, however, and had always tried to preserve their national autonomy as much as possible. To counter the Viking colonisation of Normandy and to block the initiatives of the Scandinavian/Breton alliance, Charles the Bald created a new 'march' (military region) on the eastern borders of Normandy called Neustria. This region was garrisoned by significant military forces and was under control of Robert the Strong, one of the most experienced Frankish warlords.

A Norman heavy infantryman armed with spear and sword. (Guljara Photography, © Stronghold Re-enactment)

In 866, a joint Viking/Breton force launched a massive incursion into the territory of Neustria, raiding important areas such as Anjou and Maine. Robert of Neustria responded by mobilising his troops and by asking for the help of other important French nobles (most notably of Rainulf I, Duke of Aquitaine). The Frankish military forces, mostly consisting of cavalry, succeeded in intercepting the Viking/Breton raiders before they could re-embark on their warships and go back to their bases by sailing through the River Loire. A violent pitched battle soon followed, which was a massacre for the Franks: their forces were crushed and suffered severe losses, while both Robert of Neustria and Rainulf of Aquitaine were killed.

In 867, after such a severe defeat, Charles the Bald had no choice but to come to terms with his enemies: he recognised the leader of the Bretons as 'King of Brittany' and ceded the Cotentin Peninsula to him. Despite this, the Vikings continued to ravage the valley of the River Loire during the following years: Bourges, Orléans and Angers were all sacked by them. After their previous success, the Scandinavians launched another three minor incursions against Paris during the 860s; in response to these attacks, Charles the Bald promulgated the Edict of Pistres. It was applied with a certain degree of efficiency in the Ile de la Cité, where two new fortified bridges were built to stop the longships of the foreigners (one on each side of the island, across the Seine). Paris was heavily fortified during the 870s, in view of future Scandinavian attacks; meanwhile, the Viking raids continued at scale. During 880–881, the Scandinavian warriors suffered some minor setbacks at the Battle of Thimeon (north of the Sambre River) and at the Battle of Saucourt-en-Vimeu (near Abbeville); these, however, did not change the general situation in favour of the Franks, who were still in the process of reorganising their military forces.

Siege of Paris

In 885, the Vikings decided to launch their largest attack against France, which resulted in the famous Siege of Paris. This time, 300 warships with 12,000 warriors entered the mouth of the Seine, with the clear objective of creating a permanent settlement in northern France. Odo, Count of Paris, was well prepared to receive the foreigners: he knew, in fact, that the two new low-lying footbridges in his city (one made of wood and one made of stone) blocked the passage of the Scandinavian ships. Before the arrival of the enemies, he built a tower at the bridgehead of each bridge in order to better defend his city from attack from the banks of the Seine. After reaching Paris, the Vikings demanded payment of a large sum of money. Odo refused and siege operations began. The Scandinavians attacked the north-eastern tower, which protected the bridge made of wood. They were repulsed with heavy losses by the French defenders, who employed a deadly mixture of hot wax and pitch to stop their enemies. During the following days, the Vikings bombarded the city with siege engines and tried to destroy the bridge with fire, but all their attempts failed due to the sturdy resistance of the locals.

The Scandinavians maintained the siege for two months, building trenches and raiding the nearby countryside in search of supplies. In January 886, they tried to fill the river shallows with debris and plant matter to get around the besieged tower, but ultimately decided to change strategy and set three burning warships against the wooden bridge

A Norman heavy infantryman equipped as a swordsman. (Guljara Photography, © Stronghold Re-enactment)

A Norman medium infantryman carrying seax and kite shield. (Guljara Photography, © Stronghold Re-enactment)

to destroy it. Serious damage was caused and when a few days later, rain caused an overflow of the debris-filled river, the bridge collapsed. The north-eastern tower was by now completely isolated: its remaining 12 defenders refused to surrender and were all killed by the Scandinavians. At this point the Vikings divided their forces into two parts: one remained on the eastern bank of the Seine in front of Paris, while the other sailed upriver to pillage as much as possible. Le Mans, Chartres and Evreux were all attacked by the pirates, who entered the course of the Loire River to sack urban centres.

In May 886, disease began to spread among the ranks of the city's defenders. The situation was desperate for the Franks and Odo had no choice but to abandon the city in search of reinforcements. He was later able to return to Paris at the head of a French royal army and to enter the city from the bridge made of stone. By that time, a large part of the besiegers had already decided to return home and the leadership of the Scandinavians who had remained around Paris was now in the hands of a warlord named Rollo. After another failed attack against the Ile de la Cité and after the arrival of some substantial Frankish reinforcements, Rollo finally accepted a payment of 700 pounds of silver in exchange for leaving Paris. Odo, who had been able to save the city, became King of

A Norman medium infantryman armed with an axe. (Guljara Photography, © Stronghold Re-enactment)

France in 888; Paris was safe, but the Viking raids in France continued during the following decades. They were mostly directed against Normandy, where the Scandinavians were finally able to create some permanent settlements around their naval bases under the guidance of Rollo.

In 911, in an attempt to 'regularise' the Viking presence inside the boundaries of his realm, the King of France, Charles the Simple, signed a treaty with the foreigners. Rollo was given substantial portions of Norman territory for his men in exchange for his formal submission to the kingdom of France. The Vikings had to promise that they would defend the territory of Normandy from the attacks of other Scandinavian groups and had to convert to Christianity. In practice, Rollo became a vassal of Charles the Simple in exchange for possession of a vast territory in northern France.

Belgium

During 810–884, the Scandinavians attacked the coastline of present-day Belgium and the Netherlands several times, plundering many settlements and establishing a number of permanent bases. Those regions

Armies of the Viking Age, 840–1100

A Norman medium infantryman armed with a seax.
(Guljara Photography, © Stronghold Re-enactment)

were formally and politically part of West Francia, but in practice they were abandoned to their destiny since the Franks did not have a fleet that could defend them from Viking incursions. Frisia, the northern portion of the Netherlands, was particularly exposed since it bordered the southern part of Denmark and could be attacked by the Vikings by land.

The Frisians, however, were one of the few Germanic communities of the Frankish Empire who knew how to build effective warships and had good seafaring capabilities. As a result, they organised a strong resistance to foreign pirates. An extensive system of dykes and sea walls was built in order to protect the coastline from Scandinavian landings. Despite all their efforts, however, the Frisians could not prevent the Vikings from establishing some bases on their territory.

In 850, Lothair I had to acknowledge the Scandinavian warlord Rorik of Dorestad as his vassal and as the ruler of a large portion of Frisia. During 879, a large Viking force, commanded by the Danish leader Godfrid, established a base at Ghent and rapidly assumed control over the whole of Frisia. In 884, at the Battle of Norditi, the Frisians defeated in a decisive way the Scandinavian invaders, who were surprised by the incoming tide during the retreat that followed the clash and suffered heavy losses. After this clash, the Vikings ceased to be a menace for the Frisians, who started to enjoy a higher degree of political autonomy inside the Holy Roman Empire.

Duchy of Normandy

The Duchy of Normandy was officially established in 911, when the King of France, Charles the Simple, and the Viking leader, Rollo, signed the important Treaty of Saint-Clair-sur-Epte. Scandinavians who were already settled in Normandy became vassals of the French monarch in exchange for being permitted to create their own semi-autonomous country in northern France. The Vikings were given all the Norman lands located between the Epte River and the sea, plus Brittany. Brittany had never been under the firm control of the French monarchy so, at least temporarily, the rulers of France decided

A Norman medium infantryman wearing a nasal helmet. (Guljara Photography, © Stronghold Re-enactment)

A Norman light infantryman, wearing a soft Phrygian cap and being armed with mace. (Guljara Photography, © Stronghold Re-enactment)

not to exert their authority over it. In exchange for receiving a new 'homeland' for his followers, Rollo guaranteed his loyalty to Charles the Simple and promised that his fierce warriors would protect the French territories from the incursions of any other Scandinavian group.

The Treaty of Saint-Clair-sur-Epte contained some other conditions that the Vikings had to respect: first of all, the Scandinavians were to adopt the Christian faith as their new religion; in addition, they were to respect the central authority of the French monarchs in some specific administrative fields. Considering that feudalism was developing in France during those years, the compromise found between Rollo and Charles the Simple was basically the stipulation of a 'feudal contract' between two parties that had very little respect for each other. To seal the treaty, Rollo agreed to be baptised and married Gisela – a legitimate daughter of Charles the Simple.

Over time, an increasing number of Scandinavians started to settle in the Duchy of Normandy. Initially called 'Northmen' by the French, these settlers soon started to be known as 'Normans'. The early years of the Scandinavian presence in Normandy were not easy, because the Normans had to abandon paganism and learn how to speak French. The fusion between their culture and the local one, however, soon yielded positive results; many Scandinavian warriors, for example, married French women and thus, new 'Norman' families were created. The former Vikings generally had positive relations with the French living inside and outside the borders of their territories. However, they had to fight the Bretons on several occasions since the Bretons did not accept that their country had been assigned to their former allies. Being the most war-like vassals of the French monarchy, Rollo and his warlords soon started to expand their territorial possessions by moving westward from the valley of the Seine.

In 927, the Viking leader and first Duke of Normandy was succeeded by his son William Longsword. William was favourable to the 'Gallicisation' of his followers and had a high opinion of contemporary French institutions. For these reasons, soon after assuming power, William faced a rebellion mounted by some of his warlords who wanted to preserve the Viking identity of their community. William crushed the revolt and later proved to be a capable ruler. Taking advantage of the ongoing internal conflicts that ravaged the kingdom of France, he convinced the central government to assign him some other lands that became part of the Duchy of Normandy: the areas of Avranches and of the Cotentin Peninsula (which had previously been part of Brittany) as well as the Channel Islands. The Bretons, however, continued to fight to preserve their independence and mounted a strong resistance. William and his Normans, thanks to their military superiority, won a series of clashes against the Bretons and razed to the ground most of the enemy fortifications. Thanks to William Longsword's campaigns Brittany effectively came under Norman control (albeit only for a short period). During the last years of William's rule, the Normans were heavily involved in the civil wars fought in France between various feudal lords, which usually determined the ascendancy of new monarchs. William's worst enemy was Arnulf of Flanders, who attacked the Duchy of Normandy and formed an alliance with the Bretons. Together his enemy was able to reconquer – at least temporarily – several territories that had been conquered by the Normans. William Longsword was killed in an ambush – probably organised by Arnulf – in 942.

William was succeeded by his son Richard, who later became known as Richard I. The new Norman ruler was just a boy and thus he soon came under the control of his father's enemies: Louis IV of France and Arnulf of Flanders. Arnulf wanted to eradicate the Norman presence in northern France, since it was considered extremely dangerous for the political stability of France. To most of the French aristocrats, in fact, the Normans were foreigners who had been permitted to settle in France due to the weakness of their central government. The young Richard was taken away from Normandy and was placed in the custody of the Count of Ponthieu; meanwhile, Louis IV tried to divide the Duchy of Normandy in two parts and to assign these to some of his most trusted allies.

The French monarch, however, was too weak to reconquer Normandy. The Normans, in fact, rebelled against him and obtained the release of their young but legitimate ruler. In 946, Richard I formed an alliance with the Vikings that were active in other areas of France and went to war against Louis IV. Louis IV was defeated and captured by the Normans; and released only after formally recognising Richard as the legitimate Duke of Normandy. Soon after these events, Richard I formed an alliance with the main enemy of Louis IV, Count Hugh of Paris. The Count had plans to become the new king of France and needed the support of the Normans. In 947, Richard of Normandy and Hugh of Paris were attacked by Louis of France and Arnulf of Flanders, who had been joined by Holy Roman Emperor Otto I in their anti-Norman efforts. Against all odds, Richard and Hugh prevailed; their victory led to a long period of peace and stability for the Duchy of Normandy, during which Richard I transformed his country into the most cohesive and powerful of France's feudal principalities.

In 955, the son of Hugh of Paris, Hugh Capet, became the new monarch of France. Richard I married Emma, a sister of the new king, and cemented the alliance between his duchy and the

Byzantine heavy infantryman wearing a corselet of lamellar armour over his hauberk of chainmail and aketon of padded material.
(Photo Skjaldborg Vikings, ©Ancient Armoury)

new Capetian royal family. Under Richard I – also known as Richard the Fearless, because of his courage – the 'Gallicisation' of the Normans was completed. The church, too, became increasingly powerful in Normandy, thanks to the construction of some flourishing monasteries.

In 996, Richard II, son of Richard I, became the new ruler of Normandy. The new duke was less warlike than his predecessor, and established a solid alliance with both Robert II of France and Geoffrey I of Brittany. Richard II provided the Vikings who raided England with sanctuary and permitted them to sell their plunder in Normandy. These acts clearly violated a treaty that had been signed some years before between Richard I and the Saxon king of England, Aethelred the Unready. Aethelred decided to mount an expedition against Normandy with the objective of capturing Richard II, but met with a complete failure when Saxon troops disembarking on the Cotentin Peninsula were soundly defeated by the Norman cavalry. By that time, in fact, the Normans had already adopted the standard military equipment and tactics based on heavy cavalry that were usually employed in feudal France. After these events, Richard II tried to establish positive relations with the kingdom of England, by organising the marriage of his sister Emma and Aethelred the Unready. In 1013, Richard II concluded an important alliance with Sweyn Forkbeard, King of Denmark and father of Cnut the Great; when Cnut became King of England after Aethelred's death, Richard II's sister Emma married Cnut. Emma's children included the future king of England, Edward the Confessor, and the future king of Denmark Harthacnut.

In 1026, Richard II died and was succeeded by his eldest son Richard III, who became the new Duke of Normandy. The reign of Richard III, however, was extremely brief since he had to face – immediately after his ascendancy – the rebellion of his younger brother Robert. Richard was able to crush the revolt, but died suddenly after having defeated his brother. It is highly probable that he was poisoned. After these events, in 1027, Robert became the new Duke of Normandy. He had to pacify his country after a period of internal unrest and to do this he had to replace several of the Norman nobles loyal to his brother with nobility supportive of his cause. Many of the aristocrats who were deprived of their lands in Normandy left northern France and went to southern Italy in search of fortune and a new homeland.

Robert did not have a very positive relation with the most important representatives of the church established in his duchy and confiscated many properties belonging to them. This resulted in a temporary excommunication of Robert, which did not help him in the pacification of Normandy. The new duke played a prominent role in the feudal wars that ravaged the kingdom of France, taking advantage of the weakness of the Capetian monarchy. He obtained the region of Vexin from the central government and mounted a major military campaign against Brittany. At that time, the Bretons were ruled by the energetic Alan III, who had expansionist ambitions. At a certain point in his life, Robert decided to go on pilgrimage to Jerusalem, probably with the intention of improving his relations with the church. Before leaving Normandy, he made his only son William – an illegitimate son – his heir. In July 1035, while on pilgrimage, Robert fell ill and died. The ensuing succession was an extremely complex one, since William – called 'William the Bastard' by his enemies – was just eight years old.

Until 1047, the Duchy of Normandy lived in a state of anarchy, since many of the most prominent local nobles had no intention of recognising William as their legitimate ruler. The young duke was given several different 'guardians', each of whom tried to pursue his own personal interests. In 1046, the enemies of William mounted a major rebellion and attempted to capture him; the young duke, however, fled to the Capetian court and organised the reconquest of his country with the decisive support of the King of France (Henry I) and of the church. In the early months of 1047, William and Henry won a decisive battle against the rebels near Caen; after this clash, William assumed effective power in Normandy and promulgated a 'Truce of God' with the objective of ending the feudal rivalries that had ravaged his duchy for so many years.

William soon showed he was a very capable administrator: he travelled constantly around his duchy confirming charters and collecting revenues, in order to avoid the outbreak of new feuds and to preserve the economic stability of his country. He organised his ducal household into several autonomous departments, each of which performed a specific function. William cultivated his alliance with the church by participating in councils of the clergy and by personally making the appointments of Normandy's bishops. For example, he appointed his loyal half-brother Odo as Bishop of Bayeux around 1050. Over time, William's political and military power increased; this made King Henry I suspicious and led to the formation of an alliance between the king and those Norman nobles who were still against William.

In 1054, the Duchy of Normandy was invaded from two sides by two massive enemy armies. Against all odds, however, William defeated Henry I and his internal enemies. Some minor fighting continued until 1060, but with the failed royal invasion of 1054, William's control over Normandy became absolute. In 1057, the duke repulsed another attack directed against his domains and in 1058, he invaded the county of Dreux. William was extremely ambitious and needed strong allies in France. To achieve this objective, he married Matilda of Flanders, the daughter of Count Baldwin V of Flanders. The count was one of France's most powerful aristocrats and a warlord who controlled significant military resources.

Until 1051, Edward the Confessor, the childless king of England, had very little contact with his grandson William of Normandy. During that year, however, a crisis broke out in England between Edward and the man who had been chosen as his successor on the Saxon throne – Harold Godwinson. Harold was temporarily exiled from the kingdom of England. As a result, Edward chose William instead to replace Harold as his successor. In 1051, the Duke of Normandy visited England and established a stronger relationship with Edward the Confessor. After having already enlarged his domains with the county of Dreux, in 1062, William invaded the county of Maine and after two years of campaigning, annexed it to the Duchy of Normandy. In 1064, the warlike duke invaded Brittany, with the objective of weakening the latter's ruler as much as possible. When William completed his Breton campaign, most of the local aristocrats had become loyal vassals of Normandy. By 1066, when Edward the Confessor died, William was the most powerful warlord of France and was ready to claim the English throne for himself.

Byzantine soldier wearing his civilian clothes. The decorations on the lower legs and on the shoes are clearly Byzantine. (Photo Skjaldborg Vikings, ©Ancient Armoury)

Chapter 8

The Viking Settlement of the Atlantic

The Vikings were the most important explorers of the Middle Ages, with phenomenal seafaring skills. They navigated successfully across the northern portion of the Atlantic Ocean to reach the coastline of North America after having 'colonised' the Faroe Islands, Iceland and Greenland. The explorative successes of the Scandinavians were mostly due to the exceptional quality of their longships,

A Varangian warrior equipped with sword and round shield. (Photo Gunnar, © Dominika Černá)

but also to their courage. Prior to the Vikings, no one had attempted to sail across the Atlantic in search of new lands. The Vikings believed that the world had precise limits and, when navigating westwards, thought they were moving towards the boundaries of the known lands. Their beliefs were extremely risky. Despite their ignorance, by moving from one island to the next, they surpassed the limits of medieval knowledge to find new lands of opportunities where their expanding communities could flourish.

The real protagonists of the Scandinavian explorations were the Norwegian Vikings, who were used to navigating far from their coastline and who had excellent naval bases in the fjords of their homeland. These narrow bodies of water were perfect for protecting anchored ships and for building new vessels in safety. Moving from Norway during the early decades of the 9th century, the Vikings reached the Faroe Islands, north of the Shetlands, and in a key position for exploring the Atlantic.

According to the latest research, the Faroe Islands were already inhabited prior to the arrival of the Scandinavians; although their early communities, probably coming from Scotland, were too small to be significant and thus were easily colonised by newcomers.

According to Viking traditions, the first Scandinavian to reach the Faroe Islands was a man named Grimur Kamban. It is probable, however, that he was the first to settle on the islands but not the first to discover them, since the Vikings regularly sailed across that area of the Atlantic. Over time, the Scandinavian communities living on the Faroe Islands started to flourish, successfully cultivating crops and raising livestock. The Vikings living on the Faroe Islands were peaceful farmers and not warriors: their islands were not used as bases for launching piratical raids. Collectively they adopted a 'democratic' form of government: all free men of the islands were part of a council, which made laws and solved disputes. Around the year 1000, the inhabitants converted to Christianity and in 1035, their territory officially became part of Norway. Apparently both the conversion and the annexation to Norway were the result of internecine conflict that saw the inhabitants of the northern islands attacking those of the southern ones. The history of the Faroe Islands remained linked to that of Norway for the next four centuries, seeing no major political changes.

Between the Faroe Islands and Iceland is a distance of 450 miles. It seems that Iceland had already been visited by navigators before the arrival of the Vikings. According to recent studies, some semi-permanent outposts were built on Iceland's coastline between 770 and 870. These were inhabited during summer and were probably used for fishing. Yet, before the arrival of the Scandinavians, the few navigators who travelled from Scotland and who had built these outposts had not established a permanent presence there. After having explored the coastline of the island for several years and realising that Iceland could be settled, the first Vikings landed around 874.

In a few decades they were able to cover most of the island with new rural settlements, which soon started to flourish. The first expedition probably consisted of 300 or 400 individuals, but these were soon followed by more than 20,000 people during the next decades. By the time of their arrival, the climate of Iceland was relatively warm and thus agriculture became profitable. As a

A Varangian warrior. Note the presence of a piece of chainmail protecting the face. (Photo Hrafn Vaeringi, © Amy Nicklin Photography)

result, the colonisation of the island was the perfect response to the problems of overpopulation experienced by Norway. Unlike the British Isles, Iceland could be settled easily, since there were no native communities.

By 930, the Scandinavians had completed their settlement and covered the island with 1,500 farms that were inhabited by 24,000 individuals. Just like the population of the Faroe Islands, the communities of Iceland adopted a democratic constitution and established an assembly – named Alpingi – attended by all free men. The Icelandic Vikings were peaceful individuals and capable farmers; their communities flourished thanks to naval trade. The Scandinavian communities in Iceland continued to live in peace and prosperity until 1220, when the so-called Age of the Sturlungs began.

The new age was characterised by two main elements: attempts to seize control of the island by the kingdom of Norway, and the internecine conflicts fought between the most prominent Icelandic families. It was during the Age of the Sturlungs, in 1238, that the largest battle in the history of Iceland was fought. The population of the island had grown significantly during the previous decades, to the point where warring clans were able to mobilise a total of 2,700 warriors. The Age of the Sturlungs had a very negative impact, since the wars between opposing clans reduced the economic capabilities of the island. The kingdom of Norway took advantage of this situation, annexing Iceland in 1264 as a result of the local civil wars. This political operation was carried on by the Norwegian monarch Haakon IV, who dreamed of creating a large Norwegian empire across the Atlantic by uniting the various settlements that had been established by the Vikings during previous centuries. It was Haakon, for example, who planned the Norwegian expedition against Scotland described in previous chapters and who formed a military alliance with the kingdom of the Isles. Since 1264, a new phase in the history of Iceland began and the Viking era came to an end.

Greenland

Moving from Iceland, the Vikings continued their exploration/settlement of the Atlantic coastlines by reaching Greenland. This was not an inhospitable land during the Middle Ages, since it was covered with grassland along the southern coastline and could be cultivated. Before the arrival of the Scandinavians, Greenland was populated by sparse communities of Paleo-Eskimo immigrants who travelled from North America. These people experienced serious problems settling in Greenland, but were always able to retain a presence on the island.

The Scandinavians became aware of Greenland's existence around 970, when a Viking navigator who was moving from Norway to Iceland was blown off course by a storm and sighted the coastline of the island. After the navigator finally reached Iceland, the local Vikings were informed of Greenland's existence and the first explorative expeditions started to be organised. The Scandinavian colonisation of Greenland was guided by the most famous of the Viking explorers: Erik the Red. He arrived in Iceland with his family around 950 and was the son of

A Varangian warrior armed with axe, sword and seax. (Photo Gunnar, © Dominika Černá)

A Varangian warrior armed with a sabre having curved blade. Note the excellent manufacture of the pointed helmet. (Photo Hrafn Vaeringi, © Amy Nicklin Photography)

a man who had been banished from Norway. For several years he lived as a farmer on the island, until he was involved in a bloody feud that caused his expulsion (for three years) from Iceland. According to Viking sources, Erik was banished from his new homeland around 982. At that point of his life, he had no choice but to organise an expedition to find a new land in which to live.

A few years prior, another Viking from Iceland had already established a permanent settlement on Greenland, but his attempt had failed. Erik, being courageous but also desperate, sailed towards the northern island with the hope of being luckier. His expedition rounded the southern tip of Greenland and sailed up the western coast, where he landed and where he conducted inland explorations for three years. After his three years of exile expired, Erik returned to Iceland and brought with him interesting stories about the new land he had explored. Many Icelandic Vikings, especially those living on the poorest land, were impressed by Erik's tales and joined him in an expedition intended to colonise Greenland. Erik the Red returned to Greenland in 985 with a large number of settlers at his orders. Of the 25 ships that left Iceland, however, only 14 reached their destination. Sailing in the cold waters of the Northern Atlantic was extremely difficult, particularly because the Scandinavians did not have comprehensive knowledge of Greenland's coastline.

A Varangian warrior equipped with two-handed Danish axe. The helmet has an aventail of chainmail for protection of the neck. (Photo Gunnar, © Dominika Černá)

Despite the great initial difficulties, Erik's men built two colonies in their new homeland: the Eastern Settlement (present-day Qaqortoq) and the Western Settlement (present-day Nuuk). Erik had planned to build more Viking colonies in the interior of the island, but soon realised that the two original settlements were the only areas of Greenland where farms could be established due to the relative fertility of the terrain. The interior areas were covered with snow and ice for most of the year. The early years of the Scandinavian presence in Greenland were difficult ones; the only way to have enough food was to hunt in the interior of the island. Every summer, when the weather was favourable to travel, both the Eastern Settlement and the Western Settlement sent their best men to hunt in Disko Bay above the Arctic Circle. The two groups of hunters collected large amounts of food as well as valuable produce such as seals (used to produce ropes), or ivory obtained from walrus tusks.

Erik the Red established himself in the Eastern Settlement, where he built a large estate and assumed the title of Paramount Chieftain of Greenland. He had started his career as a poor exile who had been forced to leave his homeland;

now he was greatly respected and very wealthy. The economy of the Eastern Settlement was based on livestock farming and on seal hunting; its population saw a rapid expansion and thus, by 1000, there were more or less 5,000 Viking inhabitants of Greenland. In those years, Iceland began experiencing problems of overpopulation and thus significant numbers of immigrants left their settlements to move to Greenland. In 1002, however, a group of immigrants coming from Iceland brought an epidemic that ravaged Greenland. Many of the local inhabitants died, including Erik the Red, and this time marked the beginning of the Eastern Settlement's decline. In fact, it became part of the kingdom of Norway in 1261, after its population had already converted to Christianity (1126). The Viking presence in Greenland survived until the early 15th century, but gradually became marginal due to climate change (the temperature became colder) and to the outbreak of conflicts with the Inuit communities.

The Vikings started to explore lands located west of Greenland soon after Erik the Red arrived with the first colonists and, at some point, discovered the coastline of present-day Canada. According to contemporary sources, a Scandinavian merchant, who was sailing between Iceland and Greenland, was the first to see the coast of North America after a storm during his voyage. The merchant reported his discovery to Erik the Red's son and future successor, Leif Erikson, who organised an expedition to leave Greenland for the

A Varangian spearman wearing a leather corselet of lamellar armour. (© Compagnie de la Branche Rouge)

unexplored and newly discovered land. Initially, Erik the Red participated, but ultimately chose to remain in Greenland while his son assumed command. Leif had a single ship and just 40 men at his orders; despite this, he was able to reach North America and to land on Baffin Island. After venturing further by sea, he landed on a forested tract of coastline that he called Markland. The area corresponds to present-day Cape Porcupine in Labrador. The Scandinavian explorers were impressed by the natural resources of these new lands. They were covered with woods and crossed by long rivers, home to thousands of salmon. North America was the perfect homeland for a Viking, since the abundance of trees was perfect to build ships and the presence of food reserves permitted the creation of stable settlements.

As winter approached, Leif decided to encamp on the coastline and to send out small parties to explore the surrounding areas. During their explorations, the Vikings discovered that the region was full of vines and grapes: so they called it Vinland. The area probably corresponded to the coastline of Labrador. Leif and his men built a semi-permanent settlement and left North America in spring, returning home with a cargo full of grapes and timber. When Leif returned to Greenland in the early months of 1002, he probably started planning a new expedition to establish a permanent settlement in North America but his father's sudden death and the problems experienced by his home community in that year prevented that from happening.

It was Leif's brother Thorvald, instead, who went to North America during 1004. He found the camp that had been built two years before and spent the cold months in Vinland. Thorvald was the first Viking to come in contact with the natives of Newfoundland and considered them enemies. He attacked a group of natives without reason, killing nine people. Apparently, the Scandinavians had no idea of the numbers of the native communities. A few days after these events, a large number of local warriors attacked the Viking camp and Thorvald was killed by an enemy arrow. Despite the death of their leader, the Scandinavian explorers remained in Vinland for another year before returning to Greenland.

In 1009, a new Viking expedition travelled to North America. It was commanded by Thorfinn Karlsefni and consisted of three ships transporting 160 colonists together with livestock. The previous expeditions, organised by Erik the Red's sons, had been too small to permit the establishment of a permanent settlement; now, however, Thorfinn was determined to create a permanent settlement on Newfoundland. Unlike his predecessor, he tried to establish a positive relationship with the natives. His colonisers, for example, exchanged milk and red cloth with fur and skins provided by the natives. At a certain point, however, the situation changed: the natives probably realised that the foreigners were intending to stay and thus decided to attack the Viking settlements with a large number of warriors. The ensuing fight was particularly violent, since Thorfinn's men were determined to defend their new homeland. Despite their efforts, however, the Scandinavians were defeated and forced to abandon the new positions that they had established on Newfoundland. For some time, they remained in their original camp, but ultimately decided to leave North America and return to Greenland.

The natives of Vinland and Greenland were called 'Skraeling' by the Vikings

A Varangian warrior armed with spear and axe; the latter is hanging from the waistbelt. (Photo Gunnar, © Dominika Černá)

and were extremely warlike according to Scandinavian sources; we know very little about them, but they were surely quite numerous. Their resistance was the main factor behind the failure of the Viking colonisation of Vinland. Thorfinn understood that any future settlement in North America would have been under constant threat of attack from the natives. A permanent colonisation of North America was impossible from a practical point of view: Vinland was too far from Norway or Iceland and thus any expedition aimed at exploring North America had to be organised in Greenland. The Scandinavian settlements on Greenland were too small and sparsely populated to provide a sufficient number of explorers. In addition, there was no central authority governing the exploration of new lands. Initially the Vikings hoped that Vinland could be settled without encountering opposition as it had happened for Iceland and Greenland. In North America, however, they learned that the western lands were densely inhabited by a population of warlike natives. We can only imagine what may have happened if the Scandinavian presence in Newfoundland had become a permanent one: America would have been colonised by Europeans five centuries earlier than the reality and the Vikings would have played a prominent role in this historical process. New products would have reached European markets, while the natives of North America would have been forced to face a new enemy. With the progressive decline of Greenland, the 'Atlantic empire' established by the Vikings came to an end and left behind just a few tangible elements. These were particularly significant in Iceland, which soon became part of the Scandinavian world. The short-lived history of Vinland was forgotten for long time, until archaeological finds confirmed the existence of a Viking presence in Canada.

A Varangian settler equipped as a spearman. (© Skjaldborg Vikings)

A Varangian armoured warrior, wearing lamellar cuirass and being equipped with Danish axe. (Photo Skjaldborg Vikings, © Darling Muse Photography)

A Varangian armoured warrior, carrying sword and round shield. (Photo Hrafn Vaeringi, © Amy Nicklin Photography)

Chapter 9
The Vikings in Eastern Europe

The Vikings coming from Denmark and Norway expanded into Western Europe and across the Atlantic; those based in Sweden conducted raids and exploration towards Eastern Europe and most notably Russia. The Swedish Vikings who settled in Eastern Europe were known as Varangians and were brilliant conquerors, exactly like the Vikings who terrorised the British Isles and France for two centuries. Before the appearance of the Scandinavians, Russia was mostly inhabited by various tribes of the Eastern Slavs who had settled in a very large area between the Baltic Sea in the north and the Black Sea in the south. The northern portion of this vast region was covered with dense woods, while the south consisted of vast plains, part of the immense Eurasian steppes. The whole territory of Russia was crossed by long and navigable rivers including the Volga and the Don, which were to become fundamental waterways. Their presence, in fact, enabled the Scandinavians to travel long distances in complete safety and to cross a land of which they knew very little (at least initially).

Russia was replete with natural resources and had great economic potential due to its strategic position. The lands of the Eastern Slavs, in fact, were located between the Scandinavian world in the north and the Byzantine Empire in the south. The Varangians saw Russia as a land of opportunities since there was potential to create a commercial network, carrying goods along the major rivers of the region from Scandinavia to the territories of the Byzantine Empire. The Byzantine Empire was the richest and most sophisticated state of Medieval Europe, in which a distinct civilisation had developed after the fall of the Roman Empire in the West. The Varangians soon realised that the Slavs were militarily weak, since they were fragmented into many tribes and were not particularly warlike. As a result, the Scandinavian penetration in Russia was quite easy and rapid. South of the Slavs, on the territory of present-day Ukraine, there were communities of Khazars. These were a nomadic steppe people of Turkic stock and fought mostly as mounted archers equipped with powerful composite bows; as a result, they were much more warlike than the Slavs and put up a strong resistance against the Varangians.

The expansion into Russia began around 850, in the area of the eastern Baltic located south of Finland. Here the Slavs lived together with some Finnic communities, who controlled most of southern Finland. By 859, the Varangians from Sweden had already been able to impose their rule over the Slav and Finnic tribes living near the Baltic. In 862, there was an anti-Varangian revolt, but this did not have long-lasting effects because the internal divisions between the Slav and Finnic communities prevented the formation of a solid anti-Scandinavian alliance. Shortly after the end of the revolt, the Slavs 'invited' the Varangians to their lands and become their overlords, with the hope that the foreigners could keep order and prevent the outbreak of further internecine conflicts.

Three powerful Varangian brothers, Rurik, Sineus and Truvor, the leaders of the future Rus' or 'Russi', accepted the invitation and went to Russia at the head of their retainers. They established themselves in Novgorod, not far from the Baltic Sea and on the Volkhov River, where they rapidly built an important commercial centre that connected with all the major waterways of the region. After the death of his two brothers, Rurik became the sole ruler of the Varangians and established the so-called Rurik Dynasty. It would dominate the political life of Russia during the following centuries. After the Varangians had

A detail of the armour worn by a Varangian warrior, comprising vambraces and plates for protection of the shoulders. (Photo Hrafn Vaeringi, ©Amy Nicklin Photography)

Detail of the belt equipment used by a Varangian warrior. The small bag is decorated with rich embroidery. (Photo Hrafn Vaeringi, © Amy Nicklin Photography)

secured their position in Novgorod, Rurik decided to send two of his best men to the southern regions of Russia to conduct a long-range exploration. His objective was to reach Constantinople and to open a new commercial route with the Byzantine Empire.

Askold and Dir, the two warriors chosen to explore southern Russia, were very successful in their mission: on their way south, while crossing the lands of the Khazars in Ukraine, they discovered a small but well-fortified settlement located on a hill and decided to conquer it. It would later become the city of Kiev, the most important urban centre of the Varangians in southern Russia. During the following decades, by travelling on the Dniepr River, thousands of Varangians moved from Novgorod to Kiev and so it became increasingly important commercially. The immense lands located between the two

Varangian centres were progressively settled by the Scandinavians, who easily overcame the scarce resistance of the local Slavs. Very soon the culture of the Varangians and Slavs started to meld, leading to the emergence of medieval Russia.

The rise of the Varangians was soon perceived as a menace by the Byzantines, who wanted to retain their political supremacy over the southern portion of the Balkans. The Varangians had been impressed by the tales of the foreign navigators who had visited Constantinople. They described this Byzantine capital as a city full of treasures, with churches covered with gold. As a result, the greatest ambition of the Eastern Vikings was to attack and pillage Constantinople.

In 860, Askold and Dir launched a major seaborne attack against the Byzantine capital, taking its defenders by surprise. At that time, the Byzantine military forces were fighting the Arabs in the Middle East and thus the defences of the city had been reduced. On 18 June, at sunset, 200 Varangian vessels sailed into the Bosphorus and started pillaging the suburbs of Constantinople. Encountering no opposition, the raiders moved to the nearby Isles of the Princes where they plundered local dwellings and monasteries. After having pillaged without opposition for several days, the Varangians left Constantinople before Byzantine military reinforcements could come to the aid of the city.

Rurik continued to lead the Varangians until his death. In 879; he was succeeded by Oleg, a capable warlord who acted as 'regent' for Rurik's infant son Igor. Oleg was an extremely capable military commander and since the beginning of his rule he had one main objective: preserving the unity of the Rus'. After attacking Constantinople, Askold and Dir had started to rule Kiev as an independent principality; this was unacceptable for Novgorod and thus Oleg led a large military expedition along the Dniepr River during 880–882 with the objective of restoring the unity of the Varangians.

Smolensk and Lyubech were conquered by Oleg's warriors, and Kiev was transformed into the capital of the Rus'. During the following years, the Varangian warlord Oleg created a centralised

A Varangian armoured warrior, equipped with a full set of lamellar armour. Metal plates are worn, for additional protection, on the shoulders, elbows and knees. The forearms and the lower legs are covered with strips of metal riveted together. (Photo Hrafn Vaeringi, © Amy Nicklin Photography)

A Pecheneg armoured cavalryman, armed with spear and sabre as well as a mace. The lamellar armour is distinctively nomadic. The Pechenegs, together with the Khazars, were the strongest nomadic enemies of the Varangians who had settled in Russia and Ukraine. (© Skjaldborg Vikings)

state and expanded his influence over an increasing number of Slav tribes, which were forced to become tributaries of the Scandinavians. They were obliged to provide large numbers of furs that the Varangians exchanged with the Byzantines in their markets. By 885, the subjugation of the Slavs was almost complete and the Khazars had lost the influence that they had previously exerted over Ukraine. The Rus' rapidly constructed a network of forts across their new domains and secured control over the course of the major rivers. The new state of Kievan Rus' started to prosper and soon became a major power of Eastern Europe. The Varangians exported furs, beeswax, honey and slaves on a large scale; in addition, due to the strategic position of their territorial possessions, they connected the European markets with those of Central Asia and the Middle East. The Rus' princes and merchants became extremely rich and an increasing demand for luxury goods developed in their lands.

The Byzantines tried to counter the ascendancy of the Varangians by forming an alliance with the Khazars and by establishing a military presence in southern Crimea. The Khazars supplied the Byzantines with the grain that was fundamental for the survival of Constantinople's population. These supplies came from Crimea and crossed the Black Sea before reaching the Byzantine ports.

While adopting new military measures to counter the expansionism of the Rus', the Byzantines also tried to influence the Varangians culturally by sending the missionary brothers Cyril and Methodius to Russia in 863. The two missionaries standardised the language of the Slavs by creating the so-called Cyrillic alphabet and converted large numbers of Slavs/Varangians. The increasing cultural influence of Byzantium over the Rus', however, did not change the political situation and did not stop the expansionism of the Varangians.

Every year, Oleg of Kiev collected tributes from the Slavs who were his subjects and assembled them on a flotilla of hundreds of boats that sailed down the Dniepr River in order to reach the Black Sea; after being transported to Constantinople, the Varangian products were exchanged with Byzantine luxury goods (silk, fabrics, spices, wine and fruit). The Byzantines, however, were not particularly happy exchanging luxury goods for raw materials and always tried to limit the commercial penetration of the Rus'. Under Oleg's rule, the tension between the Varangians and the Byzantines increased to the point that in 907 the Scandinavian monarch assembled an impressive fleet of 2,000 warships and attacked Constantinople.

This time, however, the Byzantines were well prepared to receive the Varangians. The gates of Constantinople were closed and the entry to the Bosphorus barred with iron chains. Oleg acted very rapidly: he disembarked with his warriors on the nearest shore and mounted wheels on his 2,000 warships, transforming them into land vehicles. When the Varangians surrounded the city walls with their dugout boats, the Byzantines were so terrified that they chose to come to terms with the attackers. Following these events, the Byzantines concluded two peace treaties with the Rus' (in 907 and 911) that had very positive terms for the Varangians.

The Varangians were permitted to establish a colony of merchants inside Constantinople and were awarded tax-free trading privileges inside the Byzantine Empire. Oleg died in 913 and was succeeded by Igor, the son of Rurik. Despite the two treaties, Igor attacked the Byzantine Empire in 941 at the head of a large fleet of 1,000 warships and 40,000 warriors. The Rus' disembarked on the northern coast

A Khazar heavy cavalryman, equipped with pointed helmet and full set of chainmail as well as with a round shield. (© Skjaldborg Vikings)

of Asia Minor, in the heart of the Byzantine Empire, where they pillaged the countryside with great violence. At that time, the Byzantine navy was fighting against the Arabs across the Mediterranean and thus the Varangians could move on the Black Sea without encountering opposition. The Byzantine defenders of Constantinople, however, were able to assemble a small naval force with 15 warships that were all equipped with throwers of the so-called 'Greek fire'. This was a combustible mixture employed as a 'secret weapon' by the Byzantines against enemy ships.

When the Varangian fleet advanced against Constantinople, the Byzantines responded by using Greek fire and destroyed several of the Rus' warships. This naval victory, however, was not a decisive one since the raiders were able to disembark and could pillage the hinterland of Constantinople. After four

A Khazar armoured horse archer, using his powerful composite bow of the steppes. (© Skjaldborg Vikings)

months of plundering in Asia Minor and Constantinople, the Varangians moved to Thrace when a large Byzantine relief force reached their positions. By that time, however, the Byzantine navy had reached the theatre of operations and could launch a surprise attack against the Rus' in Thrace. During the ensuing naval battle, the Byzantines were able to prevail thanks to the use of the Greek fire, which caused serious losses to their enemies. Igor, however, was able to escape with part of his fleet.

In 944, the Varangians returned again to Constantinople with a larger fleet, with the intention of destroying the city; this time, however, the Byzantines signed a new peace treaty, which confirmed the same terms that had been agreed in previous treaties. Igor died shortly after signing the new treaty with the Byzantine Empire. He was succeeded by his wife Olga who acted as regent for her infant son Sviatoslav. The son reached maturity in 963 and is remembered for his great military campaigns; Sviatoslav, in fact, completed the conquest of the Khazar territories in Ukraine and launched an invasion of the Balkans.

This attack took place during 967–971 and saw the Rus' fight the so-called First Bulgarian Empire. This was a very large state created by the Bulgars, a nomadic people of the steppes, in the heart of the Balkans. Over a few years, the Bulgars had become the most dangerous enemy of the Byzantines, who did not have the necessary military resources to retain control over the Balkans. In order to defeat the Bulgars, the Byzantines invited the Rus' to invade the territories of the newly-born Bulgarian Empire from the north.

The Varangians were successful and defeated the Bulgars, but very soon it became clear that they were not going to stop north of the Byzantine lands. As a result, the two victorious allies soon turned against each other and a new conflict began. For a few years, the Varangians were able to establish a protectorate over Bulgaria and in 970, a joint Varangian/Bulgarian army crossed Thrace before being defeated by the Byzantines at the Battle of Arcadiopolis. After this clash, the

A Khazar horse archer. Note the peculiar shape of his headgear and the rich decorations on his kaftan. (© Skjaldborg Vikings)

A Khazar horse archer armed with composite bow and sabre. Note the distinctive shape of the quiver. (© Skjaldborg Vikings)

Byzantines were able to reconquer most of Bulgaria and thus the Rus' decided to abandon their plans of expansion in the Balkans.

The Bulgarian Empire, meanwhile, ceased to exist as an autonomous state (at least for the moment). Sviatoslav died in 972 and his death was followed by the outbreak of violent internecine conflicts that were fought between his three sons to determine the identity of the Varangians' new leader. In 980, Vladimir emerged victorious from the civil wars that had started after the death of his father. He was the first to assume the title of Grand Prince of Kiev and played a prominent part in the process that led to the final conversion of the Rus' to Christianity.

When Vladimir died, his son Yaroslav had to struggle for power with his brothers and a new season of internal conflicts began. These ended in 1019 when Yaroslav became Grand Prince of Kiev. Like his father before him, he had to go to Scandinavia to recruit an army of mercenaries and employed them against his competitors.

Yaroslav promulgated the first law code of his realm and constructed magnificent religious buildings in his most important cities of Novgorod and Kiev. The death of Yaroslav in 1054 marked the beginning of the Rus' decline, since his three sons started to fight each other to become supreme rulers of Kiev. At the same time, the southern portion of the Kievan Rus' started to be ravaged by the Cumans, a war-like people of the steppes coming from Central Asia. Taking advantage of the Varangians' internal divisions, the Cumans defeated them at the Battle of the Alta River in 1068. The civil conflicts that ravaged Russia during this period progressively led to the fall of Kievan Rus', since the various Varangian nobles started to exert direct rule over their lands and ceased to respect the central authorities.

Many minor princedoms emerged, which were constantly at war with each other. The internal struggles also had a religious character, since many Varangian aristocrats had perceived the adoption of the Christian faith as an imposition. There was also great rivalry between Novgorod and Kiev, two 'capitals' that had competing interests but were separated by an immense distance. After 1132, the last remnants of the Rus' former unity disappeared, since the territory of Novgorod became officially independent and started to be ruled as a republic.

In 1169, the same city of Kiev was raided by a coalition of Rus' aristocrats and thus ceased to be a prominent political centre. By the end of the 12th century, the territories that had been settled by the heirs of Rurik were already fragmented into 12 major princedoms that were constantly at war with each other.

The Varangians are considered today as the real founders of Russia. Before them, the idea of a country stretching from the Baltic Sea to the Black Sea simply did not exist. Without their arrival, the Slavs would have never been able to create a centralised state like Kievan Rus'; which despite its final political fragmentation, played a prominent role in the historical process that made Byzantine culture the dominant one in Eastern Europe. It was under the Princes of Kiev, in fact, that the Varangians converted to Christianity together with the Slavs.

The Eastern Vikings were able to create a commercial empire that flourished for a long time and colonised an immense portion of Europe in just a few years. Their successes were equal in importance (if not superior) to those of the more well-known Western Vikings.

Chapter 10
The End of the Viking World

Denmark

Due to its proximity to the Holy Roman Empire, Denmark was the first area of Scandinavia where the Christian faith was introduced and where a first form of centralised kingdom was organised. During the period 960–980, Harald Bluetooth, the second King of the Danes, unified most of the petty realms existing in Denmark into a single political entity with the territory stretching from Jutland in the south to Scania in the north. Around the same time, Harald was visited by a German missionary, who convinced him and his subjects to convert to Christianity. Despite these important changes, the Vikings of Denmark continued to act as raiders and conquerors during the last decades of the tenth century, and with Cnut the Great, they reached the peak of their power. After Cnut's death, a period of internal struggles began and thus the 'modernisation' of the kingdom of Denmark was temporarily stopped.

In 1080, there was the ascendancy of a new monarch who would play a fundamental role in the history of Denmark: Cnut IV. He was a very ambitious king and a very devout one: he soon realised that the spreading of Christianity would help him exert effective control over his war-like aristocracy (which was prone to internal rebellions) and so supported the establishment of permanent religious institutions inside his realm. Cnut IV was the first Danish king to acknowledge that the glorious and violent days of the Vikings were over: England now had a strong monarchy governed by a Norman royal house, so there were no opportunities for conquering in the British Isles.

A Khazar horse archer equipped with composite bow, sabre and axe. (© Skjaldborg Vikings)

A Pecheneg horse archer firing with his composite bow. (© Skjaldborg Vikings)

During his six years of reign, Cnut IV greatly limited the power of his aristocratic warlords by stifling them and by obliging them to respect the new laws introduced by the monarchy. He introduced a series of measures that were to discourage the organisation of piratical expeditions and created a specific 'royal authority'. Cnut IV assigned to himself the ownership of common lands and the right to inherit possessions of foreign/kinless individuals when they died without heirs.

In 1085, the king assembled a large fleet with the intention of attacking England (for plundering and not for conquering); this time, however, the Danes recruited peasants and not Viking warriors. However, the fleet was not able to leave Denmark as planned and this caused great malcontent among those who had been assembled for the invasion. Instead, they revolted against Cnut IV and obliged him to flee. Gradually the rebels gained the upper hand and ultimately killed the king. Due to his support of the Church and to his violent death, Cnut was rapidly canonised and became an important figure in Danish culture. The death of Cnut IV and the failure of the expedition that he had planned effectively marked the end of the Viking Age for Denmark. During the following decades, in fact, the country became a component of Christian Europe and adopted the feudal system in a stable way. Danish society changed completely and the once warlike nobles who organised Viking expeditions became feudal lords with large territorial possessions.

Norway

Norway had some form of monarchy since 872, when Harald Fairhair became king; it should be noted, however, that he and his early successors were regarded as 'over-kings' who exerted some nominal authority over the many Viking warlords who effectively had control over the country's fjords. This situation started to change during the reign

A Pecheneg warrior armed with a peculiar kind of nomadic flail, which was employed for hand-to-hand fighting. (© Skjaldborg Vikings)

of Olaf Tryggvason, who became king in 995; he converted to Christianity before becoming monarch and later tried to spread his new religion among the many pagans of Norway. This, however, caused great malcontent among his subjects and led to the outbreak of a civil war in 999. Most of the Norwegian nobles wanted to defend their pagan traditions and had no intention of accepting the presence of a strong monarchy that could damage their interests. Olaf struggled to create a unified Norway by reducing the autonomy of the various petty kingdoms and by 'regularising' the piratical activities of his subjects. His political plans were considered potentially dangerous by the monarchs of Denmark and Sweden, who sided with the Norwegian rebel nobles during the civil war of 999. The dispute came to a head in 1000, with the Battle of Svolder that saw the defeat and death of Olaf Tryggvason.

After the clash, Norway was divided into three parts: four districts were ceded to Sweden, one district was ceded to Denmark and the remaining ones retained their autonomy despite being organised as a sort of Danish 'protectorate'.

The Gjermundbu helmet, with its distinctive eyeglass frames. (© Skjaldborg Vikings)

The years between 1000 and 1040 were characterised by continuous civil wars for Norway, which saw the participation of the Danes and Swedes on several occasions. After Cnut the Great started his military campaigns in England, the Norwegians began to resent Danish political influence over their kingdom and gradually freed their country from the control of Denmark. Olaf Haraldsson was elected king in 1015 and soon started to expel Swedes from his realm. In 1016, the decisive Battle of Nesjar was fought between the Norwegians and the Swedes, which ended with the victory of Olaf. However, he soon had to face the Danes after Cnut the Great completed his conquest of England. Incited by the King of England (who was also the King of Denmark), many Norwegian nobles rebelled against Olaf and forced him to leave Norway as an exile.

In 1030, the deposed monarch tried to regain control of his realm, but was defeated at the Battle of Stiklestad by a peasant army that was raised by the Norwegian aristocracy. Until Cnut the Great's death in 1035, Norway remained under a strong Danish political influence. In that year, however, the Norwegians rebelled against Denmark and elected Magnus Haraldsson (son of Olaf Haraldsson) as their monarch. The hostilities continued until 1040, when the new king of Norway and his Danish equivalent (Harthacnut) agreed terms. Denmark and Norway would remain two distinct realms until the death of one of them, when the survivor would unify the two countries under his rule. As a result of the above, when Harthacnut died in 1042 Magnus Haraldsson became king of Denmark. He continued the policy of his father Olaf, who had been canonised by the church, since he had two main objectives: defeating paganism and reducing the power of the Norwegian nobles.

A Viking helmet decorated with incisions on the nasal and eyeglass frames. (© Skjaldborg Vikings)

In 1047, Magnus Haraldsson died and the temporary unity between Denmark and Norway was broken. In Norway, he was succeeded by Harald Hardrada, who was the last of the great Viking monarchs. Harald was a half-brother of Magnus and had great ambitions. During 1048–64, he spent most of his time fighting the Danes with the objective of restoring the union between Norway and Denmark. When his Scandinavian plans failed, Harald turned his attention to England, which he invaded in 1066. After Harald Hardrada's death at Stamford Bridge, Norway was ruled by his two sons Magnus and Olaf until 1093. During this period, the church was permitted to establish a permanent presence in Norway and an increasing number of Norwegians converted to Christianity. At the same time, the power of the monarchy was greatly increased, since the various Viking warlords were forced to respect the new laws that were promulgated by Olaf III. The political and social transformation of the kingdom of Norway was completed by Olaf's son, Magnus Barefoot, who reigned from 1093 to 1103 and who introduced a form of proto-feudalism. Under his rule, the Viking Age came to an end in Norway.

Sweden

The first monarch in the history of Sweden was Eric the Victorious (970–995), who fought against the King of Denmark, Sweyn Forkbeard, in order to secure the autonomy of his domains. Until 970, in fact, Sweden did not exist as an independent realm and the Swedish Vikings lived under the political influence of Denmark. Eric's son and successor, Olof, initially had to accept the overlordship of Sweyn Forkbeard and even fought at his side against the Norwegians in 1000. Thanks to their alliance with the kingdom of Denmark, the Swedes obtained control over some districts of Norway and their monarchy became a stable institution.

Soon after the kingdom of Norway regained its autonomy from Denmark in 1015, however, a new war broke out between the Norwegians and the Swedes. This did not last for long and ended with success for the kingdom of Sweden, which annexed the districts of Jamtland and Halsingland that had been part of Norway until that moment. The Swedish monarchs, starting with Olof, had great difficulties in convincing their subjects to become Christians and thus Sweden was the last of the Scandinavian countries to adopt the new religion.

During 1022–60 the kingdom of Sweden was ruled by Olof's two sons, Anund Jacob and Edmund. The first was a fierce enemy of Cnut the Great and tried to break up the temporary union that was formed between Denmark and Norway. In 1026, however, he was defeated together with his allies at the Battle of Helgea. Edmund was the first Swedish monarch who planned an early colonisation of Finland and spent most of his reign trying to establish a 'balance of power' in the Scandinavian world. For example, he defined the border between Denmark and Sweden by collaborating with the Danish king Sweyn Estridsen.

Since 1060, a new royal family, the House of Stenkil, assumed control over the kingdom of Sweden; its first member, Stenkil, fought a brief but bloody war against Harald Hardrada in order to support the king of Denmark, Sweyn Estridsen. Following Stenkil's death in 1066, Sweden entered a regressive historical phase since the following kings were not able to increase the power of the central government and thus their realm continued to be dominated by the various local warlords. Around 1100, under the rule of Inge the Elder, the majority of the Swedish population converted to Christianity and the effective capabilities of the central government started to be significant ones. The expeditions of the Varangians directed towards Russia became very sporadic and – after a new brief conflict – a stable peace treaty was signed between the kingdom of Norway and the kingdom of Sweden.

By 1100, the Norse pirates and raiders who were once Vikings no longer existed, since their Scandinavian homeland had completely changed from a political and social point of

A Viking helmet of segmented construction.
(© Skjaldborg Vikings)

A Varangian pointed helmet. (© Skjaldborg Vikings)

view. However, some military institutions created by the Vikings continued to survive well after their disappearance. The most famous and important of these is the famous Varangian Guard, a Scandinavian military unit that was part of the Byzantine army. Following the end of hostilities between the Rus' and the Byzantines in 971, the diplomatic relations between Constantinople and Kiev improved. Additionally, Varangian princes married partners from the Byzantine imperial family. By that time, the Byzantine Empire was heavily involved in a series of military theatres and had great difficulties in deploying substantial numbers of soldiers on its vast Balkan frontier. Trying to solve this problem, the Byzantine monarchs decided to recruit increasing numbers of Rus' mercenaries who could serve as part of their military forces. The Varangians, like all the Vikings, were eager to fight for money and were among the most professional fighters of their age. As a result, since 970, substantial numbers of Rus' mercenaries could be found in the Byzantine Army. These were mostly deployed across the Balkans and their main task was to counter the incursions of the nomadic peoples that took place in that part of the empire.

In 987, a bloody civil war broke out inside the Byzantine territories, which forced the Emperor Basil II to ask for help from the Prince of Kiev, Vladimir the Great. Vladimir responded to the call in order to confirm the alliance existing between Kiev and Constantinople and sent a contingent of 6,000 elite warriors, who were chosen from the best Rus' fighters. The Varangians serving under Basil II played a prominent role during the Byzantine civil war and secured victory. During the period 988–999 they took part in all the military campaigns that were fought by the Byzantine army and were officially absorbed into it.

Serving in Constantinople was a dream for the Rus', who soon learned how to live the luxurious lifestyle of the Byzantines; they were paid very well by the emperor and were highly respected by their imperial commanders. Over time, the Byzantine monarchs started to rely on these courageous and audacious foreigners for their personal defence: the Varangians, in fact, were not involved (at least initially) in the political machinations of Constantinople and thus – especially in case of civil war – they always remained loyal to their emperor (meaning the person who paid them).

In 1000, the Byzantines decided to transform the Rus' warriors into an elite corps of the Imperial Guard. The old veterans sent from Kiev were organised as the legendary Varangian Guard. It soon became

A Varangian helmet decorated with incisions on the nasal area. (© Skjaldborg Vikings)

famous for its loyalty and discipline; members were armed with axes and their stature was impressive for Byzantine standards. The Varangians took part in all the major campaigns that were fought by the Byzantine Army, in every corner of the Empire; they always distinguished themselves and defeated every kind of enemy encountered on the battlefield. Service in the Varangian Guard soon evolved to become 'military apprenticeship' for young Viking aristocrats who wanted to travel the world in their youth and learn the most advanced military practices.

Around 1040, Harald Hardrada, the future King of Norway, served in the elite corps and participated in several campaigns at the orders of the Byzantine emperor. In 1071, the Varangian Guard participated in the bloody Battle of Manzikert, which saw the crushing defeat of the Byzantine army by the Seljuk Turks; many of the original Rus' warriors died in the clash, being killed at a distance by the arrows of the Turkish mounted archers. After Manzikert, the Byzantine Empire ceased to be a major military power in

Europe and the internal composition of the Varangian Guard changed considerably. Many of the fallen Scandinavians were replaced with Saxon professional soldiers who had left England after Hastings and were in search of employment. Until Manzikert, the Varangian Guard had a numerical consistence of around 6,000 warriors, but after the battle, this was reduced to just 3,000 men. The elite corps, which lost most of its original Scandinavian character after 1071, continued to exist as part of the Imperial Guard until 1204, when the city of Constantinople was conquered by westerners during the Fourth Crusade.

Gallowglasses

As we have seen in one of the previous chapters, the Viking presence in Ireland and in some peripheral areas of Scotland was very significant and led to the birth of the Norse-Gaels (individuals of mixed Scandinavian/Gael descent). These were well integrated into the Gaelic world but retained the military traditions of their Viking ancestors, such as the use of axes on the battlefield. The Norse-Gaels started to be employed as mercenary warriors by several Irish and Scottish nobles who admired their great military capabilities. As a result, many decades after the end of the Viking Age, some professional warriors continued to fight in the Scandinavian way in the British Isles. These fierce mercenaries were commonly known as Gallowglasses, by using a term that meant 'foreign warriors'. The Norse-Gael fighters came from the areas of Ireland that had been settled by the Vikings but also – more notably – from the territories of the former kingdom of the Isles and from the western coastline of Scotland. The Gallowglasses were employed on a large scale by the Irish warlords from 1260 and took part in all the most important conflicts that were fought in Ireland. Coming from Scotland and being professional fighters, they were much more reliable than most of the Irish warriors. In addition, they fought with deadly axes like their Viking ancestors and this could also be used as a 'psychological' weapon.

Most of the early Gallowglasses came from the kingdom of the Isles and were professional soldiers in search of new employment, since their homeland had been annexed by Scotland. Initially the mercenary Norse-Gael soldiers were simply paid with money, but later they were given land properties in exchange for their military services. As a result, by the time the English tried to conquer Ireland, many Gallowglasses had already settled on Irish territory and were entitled to receive supplies from the local communities. During the Middle Ages, the Norse-Gael mercenaries became a distinct component of Ireland's society and played a prominent role in slowing the English conquest of the island. They served with distinction on many occasions, being the best heavy infantry available in Ireland; most of the Irish infantrymen, in fact, were lightly equipped and the Irish aristocrats (who were rich enough to buy heavy armour) preferred fighting as cavalrymen. Being foreigners, the Gallowglasses were often employed as bodyguards by the Irish nobles and thus could exert a considerable political influence. They continued to be a fundamental component of the Irish armies until the beginning of the 17th century, when the definitive English conquest of Ireland and the spread of gunpowder weapons determined their decline. As shown by the history of the Gallowglasses, the Viking heritage in the British Isles was much more important and durable than one could imagine; during the Viking Age, in fact, most of Europe had to deal with the fierce warriors of Scandinavia.

Chapter 11
Viking Military Organisation

The Scandinavian society of the Viking Age consisted of three main classes: the *jarls* or nobles, the *karls* or freemen and the *praell* or slaves.

Nobles
The *jarls* were distinguished by their wealth, which was measured according to their personal possessions: estates, ships and goods. In addition, the power of the *jarls* was determined by the number of retainers who were at their orders. Thanks to their large territorial possessions, the Viking nobles could exert their influence over significant numbers of *karls*. Their main task was to keep order in their estates as well as to guarantee prosperity to their retainers by organising piratical expeditions across the sea. Most of the *jarls*, especially in Norway, controlled a naval base (usually located in a fjord) where their warships were built and repaired. The social position of *jarl* was hereditary, but it was not uncommon to see a *karl* becoming noble: by conducting successful raids or by serving as a well-paid mercenary. In fact, a common freeman could become rich enough to improve his social condition.

Freemen
The vast majority of the Vikings were *karls*, freemen who owned land and earned their living as farmers. Their families lived in small clusters of just three or four buildings and thus no proper cities existed in Viking Scandinavia. Each cluster usually comprised a 'longhouse', which was common property of the whole community, plus some barns and workshops. Familiar ties were particularly important and determined the social position of an individual together with his personal wealth.

Slaves
The *praell* were slaves captured during the incursions, or bondsmen. They worked in the estates of the *jarls* or in the farms of the *karls*, being treated as any other material possession. The power of a noble, for example, was determined also by the number of slaves he owned. If a Viking of any social class was unable to pay his debts, he was obliged to become a bondsman and was forced to work for his 'master' until the debt was paid. The *jarls* usually had significant numbers of bondsmen, who were forced to follow their masters during military expeditions.

A Norman nasal helmet. (© Compagnie de la Branche Rouge)

The social organisation described above determined the structure of the Viking military forces. Each *jarl* had his own *hird* or retinue of professional warriors, who were paid for their services and who had sworn their allegiance to the *jarl*. The *hirdsmen* were maintained by their noble and came from the social class of the *karls*; most of the Viking aristocrats had a *hird* of 60–120 warriors, according to their personal wealth and power. Each *hird* was commanded by an 'officer' known as *hersir*, who generally was a rich *karl* aspiring to become an aristocratic landowner.

Officers

The *hersirs* were the backbone of the Viking military forces, since they were chosen from their own community because of their combat capabilities as well as their personal influence. When a *jarl* decided to conduct an expedition overseas, it was the *hersirs* who organised the raid from a practical point of view. Each of these military commanders was at the head of 15/25 *hirdsmen*, so in each retinue there were from four to eight *hersirs*.

Hierarchy

In 885, Harald Fairhair, King of Norway, decreed that each *jarl* should have at least 80 *hirdsmen* and four *hersirs* under his command. No central military forces existed, since the kings had to count on the loyalty of their *jarls* in order to raise armies. Each monarch, however, had his own elite 'retinue' like any other Scandinavian noble. Harald Hardrada, for example, had a royal *hird* of 120 warriors; Olaf III of Norway (1068–93) doubled this and increased the number of his *hirdsmen* to 240. In time, the 'long hundred', consisting of 120 warriors, became the standard organisational unit of the Viking military forces. Each 'company' of 120 men was divided into four sub-units with 30 warriors each; these could be divided into three small groups of 10 fighters. Each sub-unit was commanded by a *hersir* and thus there were four 'officers' in each company. Each *hird* comprised two members with elite status: the *stallari* and the *merkismadr*. The first acted as a sort of 'field marshal' and was a warrior of great experience; the second acted as the standard-bearer of his retinue. With time, the internal composition of the *hirds* became more complex, since a new category of fighters appeared: these were the *gestir*, free men who did not own land properties and who received only half the pay of a standard *hirdsman*. The *gestir* appeared in Viking armies during the early decades of the 11th century; due to their lower social position, they served as light infantrymen.

The *hirdsmen* provided the bulk of the Viking military forces and were frequently paid with the money that was exhorted from the foreign communities as 'danegeld'. In addition, they shared

A Norman nasal helmet painted with two alternating colours.
(© Skjaldborg Vikings)

A Viking short-sleeved chainmail tunic with nasal helmet. (© Skjaldborg Vikings)

the booty of the incursions with their *jarls*. The jarls knew that the only way to gain the loyalty of a professional warrior was to pay him with regularity and to conduct successful piratical incursions that could lead to the capture of substantial treasure. In addition, to gain the support of the *hirdsmen*, the *jarls* provided gifts to their men. Often these had a symbolic and a material value, such as weapons or gold rings. A valiant fighter could also receive special 'prizes', such as a land property. The Vikings considered courage in battle as the most important virtue that a man could have and sometimes freed their slaves if they showed great valour in combat.

The Scandinavian society of the Viking Age was mostly an agricultural one, since most of the free men were farmers who produced corn and had cattle; between ploughing and harvest time, the *karls* took part

A Viking short-sleeved chainmail tunic with sword. (© Skjaldborg Vikings)

in commercial/piratical expeditions organised by their nobles. As a result, it would be wrong to consider plundering as the only or main component of Viking economy. The *hersirs* played a prominent role in the Scandinavian military organisation, since they were farmers like the men under their command but also had superior military skills. On most occasions the 25/35 warriors commanded by a *hersir* corresponded to the crew of a warship and thus the *hersir* was also the captain of their vessel. Providing gifts and promising booty were the only ways for a *hersir* to raise an effective war band with at least 30 fighters.

The small groups of warriors commanded by a *hersir* were characterised by the existence of a special relationship between their members, since all the fighters of a retinue were 'brothers-in-arms' and had sworn loyalty to their *jarl* over the hilt of their sword. The military system based on the *hird* was common to the entire Viking world, with the only difference that the retinues of the Varangians (Eastern Vikings) were known as *druzhinas*. As noted above, during the last phase of the Viking Age the traditional *hirdsmen* started to be supported by some *gestir* or 'guests', free men of lower social status who served as light infantrymen. These also performed a series of 'auxiliary' roles such as policing the countryside or collecting taxes from their *jarl*'s subjects.

The military system based on retinues, or war bands, was used to assemble the troops that were needed for overseas expeditions; in case of foreign attack against their homeland, however, the Vikings employed a different system of mobilisation that was known as *leidang*. Each *jarl* was obliged to provide ships and crews at his own expense if these were needed by his king. In time the *leidang* started to organise massive offensive operations, such as invasions of a foreign land, and thus partly lost its initial 'defensive' nature.

The territories of the three Scandinavian kingdoms were all divided into districts and each, according to its population and economic capabilities, had to provide and maintain a certain number of warships that were to serve under command of the central authorities when needed. The *leidang* or 'naval conscription' system existed in all the Scandinavian countries, but each realm had its own peculiarities.

Danish Territory

In Denmark, the national territory was divided into *skipen* or ship-districts, each of which was to provide a warship. Each district was divided into harbour-districts that were to provide one sailor/warrior each. Usually, the naval conscription worked according to a rotation system and thus the various ship-districts had to provide their vessel only every four years.

Norwegian Territory

In Norway, the national territory was divided into counties that were sub-divided into coastal districts. Each was to provide a warship and 40 crews in case of mobilisation.

Swedish Territory

The territory of Sweden was divided into six regions; five of these had no outlet to the sea and were divided into territorial units known as 'hundreds', while the remaining one (comprising the entire coastline of the country) was divided into ship-districts. Each of the hundreds and of the ship-districts was to provide four warships and 100 sailors/warriors (Swedish ships were smaller than the Danish/Norwegian ones and had crews of 25 rowers). The conscript forces were responsible for homeland defence and thus also performed auxiliary functions such as patrolling the coastline and transmitting warnings with beacon-chains.

Changing Power Structure

When the power of the Scandinavian kings started to be significant, from the early decades of the 11th century, the 'naval conscription' system began to be employed in order to muster large invasion forces. The army that Harald Hardrada led to England during 1066, for example, mostly consisted of conscript warriors and not of *hirds*. In any case, these 'general' mobilisations never involved all the able-bodied freemen of a country. Usually only one or two out of three individuals were called to serve at a time since a substantial labour force had to remain at home in order to work in the fields. Those men who were not mobilised had to work in the fields of the warriors called to serve. A full mobilisation (*full-leidang*) was quite rare to see, since on most occasions the kings preferred to employ a half mobilisation (*half-leidang*).

A Byzantine corselet of armour used by the heavy infantry. (© Skjaldborg Vikings)

Finally, it should be remembered that the conscript warships were usually available for royal service only for short periods of two to four months.

A growing number of Viking warriors started to sell their military services to the various *jarls* as professional mercenaries. These became increasingly important in the Viking military system from the last decades of the 10th century and were frequently organised into 'brotherhoods' with a distinct pagan nature. The most famous of these mercenary groups was that of the *Jomsvikings*, who fought for any Viking leader who was rich enough to pay them. The *Jomsvikings* had their main base at Jomsborg, on the southern coast of the Baltic Sea, from where they organised their expeditions. The senior members of the brotherhood were extremely selective in deciding whom to admit to their mercenary organisation. Membership was restricted to warriors of proven valour aged 18–50, who had to fight a duel with one of the *Jomsvikings* in order to show their combat capabilities.

All the components of the brotherhood had to respect a strict code of discipline, which was based on severe punishments. Blood feuds between members of the group were prohibited and all *Jomsvikings* were forbidden to flee from the battlefield. All captured spoils were to be equally distributed among the entire brotherhood and no member was permitted to leave the stronghold of Jomsborg for more than three days. The *Jomsvikings* were probably created by Harald Bluetooth (King of Denmark during 958–986) and became increasingly powerful. According to contemporary sources, at the height of their power they could deploy a total of 30 warships. In 984, the *Jomsvikings* tried to conquer Sweden for one of their leaders but were defeated by Eric the Strong, the first King of Sweden. Two years later they attacked Norway, being always in search of a realm to conquer, but they were also defeated on this occasion. The two defeats of 984 and 986 marked the beginning of the decline for the *Jomsvikings*, who were now perceived as a menace rather than a resource by the Scandinavian monarchs. By the 980s, in fact, the mercenary brotherhood was strong enough to menace the stability of the Scandinavian realms;

in addition, the *Jomsvikings* were the last and strongest defenders of Viking paganism. Considering them as a potential threat for the 'modernisation' of his kingdom, Magnus I of Norway decided to attack them in 1043. Jomsborg was destroyed by the king's military forces and most of the *Jomsvikings* were killed.

Berserkers

The Scandinavian military forces of the Viking Age comprised a special category of elite warriors, the *Berserkers*. They were part of religious brotherhoods that had a distinct military character and were well known for their capacity of fighting with trance-like fury. The *Berserkers* honoured some wild animals that were central in the pagan religion of the Norse and tried to emulate their combat skills. For this reason, they wore no armour and covered their bodies just with the skin of the animal that they honoured. The same term Berserker meant 'bear-shirt', because these elite warriors used to wear coats made out of a bear's skin. The traditions related to the *Berserkers* were extremely ancient and originated from the hunts of the early Scandinavian communities. Three main animal cults were practised by the Vikings: that of the bear, that of the wolf and that of the wild boar. Bear-warriors, wolf-warriors and boar-warriors all had some fundamental characteristics in common. In battle they were subjects to fits of frenzy, howled like wild beasts, foamed at the mouth and gnawed the iron rim of their shields. According to popular belief, during these 'attacks of frenzy' they were immune to steel and fire. While fighting against the enemy, the *Berserkers* assumed the combat capabilities of the animal they honoured and thus had a supernatural tendency to kill.

Contemporary Scandinavian sources used the expression 'to go berserk' to indicate the moment in which these warriors 'changed form' and entered a state of wild fury. We don't know how the *Berserkers* were able to enter a state of trance during battles, but probably they were a mixture of psychopaths and of sufferers from paranoia who were sent to the frontline in order to terrorise the enemy. Judging from contemporary sources, they were not numerous, but their appearance on the battlefield could decide the outcome of a clash: they had the physical strength of madmen and were impervious to pain. Before the spreading of Christianity, the *Berserkers* were part of the pagan kings' bodyguards and were highly prized as a result of their 'supernatural' powers. Harald Fairhair and several other Viking kings employed

Above left: A Viking round shield. (© Skjaldborg Vikings)

Above right: A Viking round shield. (© Skjaldborg Vikings)

them as 'shock troops', until paganism was gradually banned from Scandinavia. According to the latest research, it is possible that part of the *Berserkers* could reach hysteria by performing a ritualistic process known as *effektnummer* that included shield biting and animalistic howling.

Ships

Naval warfare was a fundamental component of the Viking world: ships were not just a means of transport but also a symbol of power, since control of the sea routes was a key element behind the success of a Viking community. Before the advent of sail, the Norse people employed simple rowing ships that could navigate along the coastline. With the 'Sail Revolution' of the early Viking Age, new models of ships were developed and the Scandinavians could set out across the open sea. Manufacturing large quantities of sails was a challenge for medieval communities, since spinning and weaving wool to make sails required important economic resources and a consistent labour force. Yet, the advantages given by the introduction of the sails were so significant that the Norse communities soon changed their ship building in order to mount sails on their vessels. This revolution was made possible by the invention of the keel, which permitted the development of the famous 'longship'.

The clinker-built wooden vessels with keel, oars and sail of the Scandinavians were going to conquer the world: they could maintain an average speed of 4–5 knots under oars and a maximum speed of 20 knots under sail, something incredible for the standards of the time. They could be operated in very shallow waters due to their flat keel and thus were perfect to sail on rivers. In addition, they could be easily landed on sloping beaches. Their rudder, which reached far below the keel, could be pulled up to avoid damaging it on the seabed; as a result, Viking ships could be moved out of reach of enemy ships since the enemy was unable to follow them into shallow waters.

The longships had some superior technological features, which made them extremely resistant; for example, they had a shock-absorbing inlay between the bow and the keel (which could be easily removed if damaged). The shallow keel was perfect to transport horses, something that William the Conqueror used to his advantage during the 1066 invasion of England. The great manoeuvrability and flexibility of the Viking ships made them reliable and seaworthy in every climatic condition. Being lighter and faster than enemy vessels, the longships were practically impossible to defeat during sea battles and could be deployed into different tactical formations according to circumstances. The combination of oars and sail gave the Vikings an incredible superiority over their enemies.

A Viking round shield. (© Skjaldborg Vikings)

Scandinavian ships could belong to three main categories: *knarrs* or cargo ships (bigger and broader vessels specifically designed for transporting goods and heavy freight), *karvs* or barges (small boats used for sailing between islands and skerries), and longships. Longships had a steering oar at the starboard side of the aft stem, a big rectangular sail and several fixed thwarts above the deck. The Viking longships were also known as *drakkar* or *dreki* since they frequently had carvings of animal heads (most notably of dragons) at the stem. These carved heads were usually mounted for combat and were painted with bright colours. Ships employed for military service were easy to recognise due to the presence of shields hanging along their sides (which were attached to a rope that was tied to the rim of the vessel). These shields were part of the ship's fittings and not of the rowers' personal equipment; they were used for protection from enemy arrows.

Chapter 12
Viking Military Equipment and Tactics

The Vikings were famous for the high quality of their weapons, which had a specific social function in Scandinavia during the early Middle Ages. Bearing arms was both a right and a duty of free men and distinguished them from slaves. As a result, weapons were literally status symbols and their quality and ornamentation reflected the economic capabilities of their owner. Most of the Viking warriors gave a name to their weapons and had a special connection with them, treating them as amulets with their symbolism strongly linked to the soul of their owner. Elegant shapes and rich ornamentation were typical of the aristocrats' weaponry, but most of the middle-class warriors had no hesitation in spending large sums of money on the best arms.

In Viking Scandinavia, the processes of forging and tempering were performed by specialised craftsmen and the process was surrounded by a web of myth. Use of the best materials and control of the temperatures during the various productive phases were key factors behind the creation of an effective weapon. Viking arms were often decorated with symbols that had a religious or cultural meaning; these were reproduced as patterns and inlaid into the iron during forging to became visible when the external surface of the weapon was polished and etched.

A Viking round shield with two models of seax of different length. (© Compagnie de la Branche Rouge)

Axes

The axe originally developed from the tool that was employed for working in the woods, which was originally a massive tool. Around 950, working axes and battle axes became two distinct objects, with working axes becoming lighter and narrower. In combat the Vikings employed their axes mostly to break enemy lines like 'shield-smashers'.

Three different kinds of axe were produced and each had some distinctive peculiarities. Narrow-bladed axes had a blade length of 5–10cm and were mostly employed as working tools; those having a two-handed wooden shaft were known as *boloks* and were used for fending trees. The narrow-bladed axe was not specifically designed for combat use, but since it was the only axe owned by many of the poorest free men, it was not uncommon to see it on the battlefield. Broad-bladed axes had a blade length of 20–30cm and were specifically designed

Two examples of Norman kite shield. (© Skjaldborg Vikings)

for combat use; their head could be L-shaped or M-shaped. The blade was thin but wide and had pronounced 'horns' at both the toe and the heel of the bit. These characteristics were common to the narrow-bladed axes but they were not as thin as the battle axes. L-shaped axes tended to be smaller and had the toe of the bit swept forward for superior shearing capability. M-shaped axes were bigger and had more symmetrical toe and heel.

Most of the battle axes were built with wrought iron but had a reinforced bit made of carbon steel that was placed near the edge to have a devastating cutting capability. The average weight of a Viking battle axe was 1.5kg; the wooden haft had a standard length of 1 or 1.5 metres and was linked to the head with a cap that protected its terminal part from the rigours of combat. On most occasions, the haft was obtained from ash or oak. Both the narrow-bladed axe and the broad-bladed axe were employed as double-handed weapons and were not designed for throwing. The *bearded axe* or *skeggox* was single-handed and was mostly employed as a throwing weapon. Its name derived from the hook or 'beard', ie, the lower portion of the head's bit that extended the cutting edge below the width of the butt (providing a wide cutting surface while keeping the overall weight of the weapon low). The peculiar design of the bearded axe allowed its user to grip the haft directly behind the head, something that was of great use when throwing the weapon.

Swords

Swords were much more expensive and complex to produce than axes and were generally used only by the most prominent warriors. The Viking sword was a single-handed weapon that was designed to leave one of the warrior's hands free in order to hold the shield. When employing two-handed axes, instead, Viking warriors had to carry their shields on their back. Scandinavian swords could be single-handed or double-handed (the latter being much more common than the former); their hilt consisted of three parts: back-hilt, grip and fore-hilt. The fore-hilt could be made up of two parts, the hindmost one being commonly known as the pommel. Most of the hilts were made of iron, but sometimes they could be obtained from bronze.

A good sword blade had to be flexible but should not be easily broken and its edge had to retain its sharpness for as long as possible. These main characteristics were obtained by placing hard steel on the sword's edge and soft iron along the middle of the blade. Producing a sword of good quality was

A Viking sword and scabbard. (© Skjaldborg Vikings)

A Viking sword and scabbard. (© Skjaldborg Vikings)

an extremely long process, which had many phases: forging, folding, hammering and forging again. Re-working steel and iron at high temperatures rendered them homogenous and thus reduced the risk of the weapon shattering under the strain of use.

The total length of a Viking sword was of 90–95cm, while the average length of the blade was 75–80cm. Blades were 5–6cm wide and their weight was restricted towards the point; this was obtained by tapering the single blades both in breadth and in thickness towards the point. As a result, blade thickness was 6mm near the hilt and 2mm at the point of the sword. To reduce the weight further and to increase flexibility, a groove was forged and ground out along the middle of the blade. The centre of gravity of the weapon was near the hilt and this made it quite easy to handle. Many Viking swords, especially those belonging to the richest individuals, had decorative inscriptions on the blade and decorated hilts. All swords were carried in leather-bound wooden scabbards that were suspended from a strap across the right shoulder. Like the scabbard, the hilt was made of an organic material such as horn or antler. The swords had such an important symbolic and material value for the Vikings that they were usually passed from one generation to the next; in addition, several prominent warlords chose to be buried with their sword. Most of these buried swords had their blade bent to deter robbers from violating the graves to steal such costly weapons.

Spears

The spear was the weapon of poor warriors. It was very easy to produce and was carried by the majority of common fighters. Scandinavian spears were produced in two main versions: throwing spears and thrusting spears.

The heads of the throwing spears had an average length of 20cm, while those of thrusting spears had a standard length of 70cm. Spear heads consisted of two parts: the blade and the socket. The wooden shaft was fixed into the socket with one or two nails; sometimes Viking spears could also have two projections on the side of the socket that were known as wings and which aided their removal from enemy shields. Occasionally the back end of the shaft was capped with a metal ferrule. Spear blades could be of two different kinds, the first of which was older than the second. The first model of blade was forged with a herringbone pattern along the middle and had curved edges; it blended inconspicuously into the socket. The latter tended towards a square internal cross-section and was decorated with longitudinal grooves. The second model of blade had nearly straight edges (which ended in an angle at the base) and a marked narrowing as it merged into the socket. The latter was round in cross-section and was decorated with inlaid precious metal. Wings were very common on the first model and quite rare on the second one.

The wings had another important practical function, they could be used for hooking on to the edge of an enemy shield and thus for 'opening the way' to a strike.

The wooden shaft of the thrusting spear was longer than that of the throwing spear; the former was 2.5 or 3 metres long, while the latter was 1.5 metres long. The diameter of all shafts was of 2.5cm, sometimes narrowing towards the back end. Throwing spears were less popular than thrusting ones.

Battle Knives

In addition to their axes, swords and spears, the Viking warriors sometimes also carried a long battle-knife known as *sax*; this was single-bladed, having a curved back and a straight edge. Its total length was 70–90cm, thus it was comparable to smaller swords. The handle of a *sax* was 15–25cm long and was made of wood. This short weapon was carried across the front of the lower abdomen, hung horizontally from the warrior's belt. The cutting edge faced upward, with the handle conveniently placed for the user's right hand. The *sax* was copied by the Vikings from the Saxons and was popular among the Western Vikings. The Varangians, instead, had shorter battle knives with a back and edge that were both straight.

Bows

Bows were popular among Viking warriors; they were employed for both hunting and warfare and were a common object that could be found in most Scandinavian houses. Viking bows were made from yew, ash or elm. They had a draw force of 100lbs and an effective range of 200 metres. Technically, they were 'longbows',

A Norman sword and scabbard. (© Skjaldborg Vikings)

A display of Viking swords; note the different designs of the pommels. (© Compagnie de la Branche Rouge)

since they were obtained from a single piece of wood. The overall height of a Viking bow generally corresponded to that of its user. When not in use, a Scandinavian bow was almost straight. When strung, it was nearly D-shaped in cross-section. Arrowheads could be of three different kinds: blade-shaped, spike-shaped and chisel-shaped. The second model was that specifically designed for combat use, since the other two were employed for hunting. Each arrowhead was fixed with a tang to its shaft, which was made of wood, had feathers applied on the back and was 65–75cm long.

Shields

The most important component of a Viking warrior's defensive panoply was his shield. It had a distinctive round shape and was quite flat, having a hole in the middle where a wooden carrying handle was mounted crossways on the inside. A dome of plate iron, the boss, was nailed over the hole on the outside in order to protect the hand. Viking shields had a diameter of 80–95cm and were made up of seven or eight planks glued together edge to edge in order to form a single plate. The thickness of the planks was 7–8mm near the middle of the shield and 5–6mm near the edge. A layer of rawhide was glued on to the shield's front and back and was held in position by stitch holes that were placed round the edge where a band of rawhide was folded around and sewn for reinforcement. The presence of the rawhide reduced the risk of the wood splitting and helped to stop enemy arrows. Pine and spruce softwoods were usually chosen to craft shields. Bosses could have a notched edge or a crenellated metal band set over the edge. Viking shields were frequently reinforced with an iron strip around the rim, which was particularly useful during hand-to-hand fighting. Most of the round shields were painted in a single colour, but several were decorated with specific designs. Simple crosses and derivations of sun wheels were the most common designs, together with sacred animals or creatures like dragons. The average weight of a Viking shield was 7kg. When not fighting, Scandinavian warriors carried their round shields on their back, with a leather belt that was attached to the wooden handle.

Helmet

The defensive equipment of a Viking warrior was completed by his helmet and by his armour. These were very costly and only the richest individuals or professional warriors could afford them. Early Scandinavian helmets belonged to the so-called *spangenhelm* type, since they consisted of four iron plates nailed together with metal strips that formed a sort of frame. The term *spangen*, in fact, meant 'braces' or 'strips'. This kind of helmet had a conical conformation that curved with the natural shape of the head and culminated in a point on the top. The point could be spiked and was frequently adorned with coloured feathers. The front of the Viking *spangenhelm* usually included a half 'facial' mask consisting of a loose nose-protector attached to two metal stripes designed to cover the profile of the eyebrows. The shape of the eye protection resembled that of modern eyeglass frames and thus the helmets with a half 'facial' mask are also known as 'spectacle helmets'. Full facial masks were quite rare to find. Sometimes metal cheek-plates and a neck protector made of chainmail could be applied to this model of helmet. The facial mask and the frame could be made of bronze or brass and could be heavily decorated with incisions. A magnificent surviving example of a Viking *spangenhelm* is the so-called Gjermundbu Helmet, which has a quite round shape instead of a conical one.

The helmet described above evolved into one obtained from a single piece of iron. The new helmets, commonly known as 'nasal helmets', had the same conical shape and point as the previous ones but did not have spikes. Instead of the half 'facial' mask, they had a simple nasal protector, which was sometimes attached to a ridge running around the bottom edge of the helmet. The 'nasal helmets' became popular during the late Viking Age and were later used by the Normans. The famous helmets with horns, reproduced in many depictions of the Vikings from the Romantic period, are a modern invention; some examples of bronze horned helmets are known, but these date back to the Nordic Bronze Age and were used only during ceremonies.

Armour

The great majority of the Western Vikings who had armour wore chainmail, ie, a protection for the torso obtained from a web of small iron rings. This 'coat of mail' had a very high cost similar to that of a shield, spear, sword and helmet. As a result, only the richest warlords and the professional warriors could afford

A Viking seax short sabre. (© Skjaldborg Vikings)

A Viking seax short sabre. (© Skjaldborg Vikings)

one. Half of the rings of a chainmail shirt were closed, while the others were open since their ends had to be nailed together in order to close the circle. Due to these technical features, producing a coat of mail was a work of precision that required the use of several specialised tools. Thousands and thousands of rings had to be inter-connected in order to create a single chainmail. Chainmail could be produced in a short version (*stuttr*) or in a long version (*sidr*). The first stopped at hip level and was short-sleeved, while the latter reached to the mid-thigh or as far as the knees and was long-sleeved.

The Eastern Vikings, especially those of Kievan Rus', preferred using lamellar armour. This consisted of hundreds of oblong iron plates that were laced together with straps or sewed to a stout fabric/leather shirt. The majority of the lamellar cuirasses covered only the torso, but some of them could be extended down over the hips and thighs. Sometimes the shoulders and the upper arms could be covered. The *lamellae* could be reinforced by a mid-rib and could also be decorated with gold or silver. The members of the famous Varangian Guard were mostly equipped with lamellar armour, like the rest of the Byzantine Army.

The majority of the Vikings were not rich enough to have chainmail or a lamellar cuirass; as a result, they wore textile armour obtained from organic materials that was very cheap and easy to produce. This consisted of several layers of padded cloth and could be as thick as 1cm; though this was usually worn also by the richest warriors, under the chainmail or lamellar cuirass. Linen, hemp canvas and woollen felt were usually employed to produce textile armour, which was reinforced by parallel rows of stitches running through all the layers.

Fighting Formations

Generally, the Vikings preferred fighting in tight formations stretched out in lines, in order to overlap their shields and to form a 'defensive wall' in case of enemy attack. A line could be dense or sparse, depending on how long it had to be and on how many warriors were available. The depth of a defensive formation was usually between five and eight lines. The most experienced and better equipped warriors were deployed in the front line, since the main task of those in the back lines was to plug gaps in the front line. Shoulder-to-shoulder 'shield walls' were an effective defensive formation, especially when supported by a certain number of archers; the latter, in fact, could fire their arrows from behind the round shields of the warriors equipped with spears. Like the Germanic peoples, the Vikings defended in line and attacked in column.

An attacking column usually consisted of 30 men, since it was six men long and five men deep; its numerical composition corresponded to that of a warship's crew. When attacked, a single column could be rapidly transformed into a 'shield column' if the warriors in its outer ranks overlapped their shields as

The point of a Viking spear; the two wings were designed to facilitate the extraction of the weapon. (© Compagnie de la Branche Rouge)

a wall around the whole column. When the impact with the charging enemy was imminent, the warriors in the front rank squatted down to hold their shields upright on the ground while those in the second rank held their shields above the warriors squatting down. The inside ranks covered the top of this effective 'tortoise' formation.

When attacking, a column was deployed in a very aggressive tactical formation known as *svinefylkring* or 'boar's snout'. This was a wedge formation, working in a very simple but effective way: it had the shape of an equilateral triangle, with the commander being the vertex. The best warriors were deployed near the vertex, while those with little combat experience were placed on the back of the formation. The chosen warriors of the first ranks followed the movements of their commander very closely and were in turn followed by the warriors of the other ranks; as a result, the formation could move very rapidly and was extremely flexible. If stopped by the resistance of the enemy, the attacking wedge rapidly turned into a more solid rectangle since the warriors of the back ranks advanced to support those who were near the vertex. The *svinefylkring* was perfect to attack an enemy 'wall of shields' in a precise point, but was exposed to counter-attacks on the flanks. After breaking the enemy line, the wedge formation attacked the opponents, half on the right and half on the left from the rear.

All movements were coordinated due to the presence of musicians and standard bearers on the battlefield. Musicians first played long horns to transmit orders, standard bearers indicated the position of the formation's leader with their standards. The Scandinavian military forces carried small triangular banners as well as impressive standards of the *draco* type (which produced a terrifying noise when the wind moved them). In the Viking world, horses were not used for military purposes and cavalry troops did not exist; they were, however, a status symbol and a means of transport for those few nobles rich enough to own one of them.

Norman Armour

The Norman *milites* (knights) of the period covered in this book were all protected by a *hauberk* or shirt of mail, which was made of several thousands of interlocking metal rings. The dimensions of each *hauberk* could vary considerably, since the sleeves may finish at the elbow or be a full arm's length.

Above left: **The point of a Viking spear.** (© Skjaldborg Vikings)

Above right: **A detail of a two-handed Danish axe.** (© Skjaldborg Vikings)

The lower part of a *hauberk* generally reached the knees, but could be longer or shorter. Producing this kind of armour was a long and costly process, which only nobles could sustain.

By the second half of the 12th century, the personal protections of a knight included other elements made with mail, like the *chausses* (armour protecting the legs) and the gloves. At that time, separate coifs of mail for protection of the head were not yet in use and the portion of chainmail protecting the head/neck was simply part of the *hauberk*. The chainmail was worn over a padded garment known as an *aketon*, which offered additional protection to its wearer.

The standard helmet of the Norman knights was the conical one with nasal protection, but a semi-spherical version incorporating a full facial mask became increasingly common to find. The skull of a nasal helmet could be raised from a single sheet of iron or be of composite construction. The nasal was fully integrated into either the skull or browband of the helmet. It was usually riveted to the skull or was part of a T-shaped piece protecting both the nose and the eyebrow. During the 12th century, the skull of the nasal helmets became more varied: it could have a forward-deflected apex (resembling the shape of a 'Phrygian cap') or it could be round-topped. During the last decades of the 12th century, due to the increasing diffusion of the crossbow on the European fields of battle, most of the knights started to abandon their previous helmets with no protection for the face (except for the nasal) and replaced them with new ones using different patterns of facial masks. Face masks were fixed and gave protection only to the frontal part of the face.

Norman Shields

The standard shield of the Norman 'milites' was the so-called 'kite shield', which was specifically designed for cavalry use and gave a high degree of protection to its users. Almond-shaped, it was made of laminated wood and was covered with stretched animal hide that could be painted to reproduce different decorative motifs. A band of metal was placed on the external edge of the shield for reinforcing it and – corresponding with the handle – each kite shield had a round metal reinforcement on the front known as 'umbo' (this boss could be pointed in order to be used as an offensive weapon during close combats). Kite shields were usually equipped with 'enarmes' (leather gripping straps) on their back, which gripped them tightly to the arm even when their users relaxed their arms. They also had an additional long strap that allowed them to be slung over one shoulder when not in use. The standard dimensions of a kite shield corresponded to the approximate space placed between a horse's neck and its rider's thigh; the narrow base of the shield protected the rider's left leg and the pronounced upper curve protected both the left shoulder and the torso of the rider. Due to the peculiar features described above, the kite shield was perfect for cavalry use and was much more effective than the previous round shield.

Norman Spears

The main offensive weapons of the Norman knights were the spear and the long sword. Norman spears were produced in two main versions: throwing spears and thrusting spears. The heads of throwing spears had an average length of 20cm, while those of thrusting spears had a standard length of 70cm. Spear heads consisted of two parts: the blade and the socket. The wooden shaft was fixed into the socket with one or two nails; sometimes spears could also have two projections on the side of the socket known as 'wings', which were used to easily remove the spear from enemy shields. Occasionally the back end of the shaft was capped with a metal ferrule.

A Viking short knife with incisions on the blade. (© Skjaldborg Vikings)

Spear blades could be of two different kinds. The first blade model was forged with a herringbone pattern along the middle and had curved edges. It blended inconspicuously into the socket. The second blade model had nearly straight edges (which ended in an angle at the base) and a marked narrowing as it merged into the socket. Wings were very common on the first model and quite rare on the second one. Wings could be used for hooking on to the edge of an enemy shield and for opening the way to a strike.

The wooden shaft of the thrusting spears was longer than that of the throwing spears; the former was 2.5 to 3 metres long, while the latter was 1.5 metres long. The diameter of all shafts was of 2.5 cm and sometimes narrowed towards the back end. Throwing spears were less popular than thrusting ones, since the Normans were the first knights in feudal Europe to start using their thrusting spears tucked under the armpit during frontal charges. Thanks to the employment of the stirrups, and of solid saddles with tall pommels, the Norman 'milites' could remain stable on their horses while thrusting with the spears placed under their armpits. Before the widespread adoption of stirrups, the cavalry contingents of antiquity wielded their spears overarm and thus could not employ them for thrusting with great power.

Norman Swords

Swords were much more expensive and complex to produce than spears. The Norman sword was a single-handed weapon that was designed to leave one of the warrior's hands free to hold the shield. Their hilt consisted of three parts: back-hilt, grip and fore-hilt. Sometimes the fore-hilt was made up of two parts, the hindmost one of which was commonly known as a pommel. Most of the hilts were made of iron, but sometimes they could be obtained from bronze. The total length of a Norman sword was of 90–95cm, while the average length of the blade was of 75–80cm. Blades were 5–6cm wide and their weight was restricted towards the point; this was obtained by tapering the single blades both in breadth and in thickness towards the point. As a result of the above, blade thickness was 6mm near the hilt and 2mm at the point of the sword. To reduce the weight further and to increase flexibility, a groove was forged and ground out along the middle

A Viking wooden longbow with quiver. (Photo Gunnar, © Dominika Černá)

of the blade. The centre of gravity of the weapon was near the hilt and this made it quite easy to handle. Many swords, especially those belonging to the richest individuals, had decorative inscriptions on the blade and decorated hilts. All swords were carried in leather-bound wooden scabbards that were often suspended from a strap across the right shoulder. Like the scabbard, the hilt was also made of an organic material like horn or antler.

The poorest feudal infantrymen had no military equipment to speak of: they went to war in their ordinary clothes and were mostly armed with their agricultural tools. The luckiest of them had a padded *aketon* and a simple helmet (usually of conical shape). The quilted *aketon* – the armour of the poor – was popular among the archers who were part of the feudal infantry. It was usually made of linen or wool, with the stuffing obtained from different materials such as scrap cloth or horse hair. Quilted hoods for protection of the head were usually worn together with the *aketon*.

The archers of the Norman period were equipped with bows made from yew, ash or elm. These had a draw force of 100lb and an effective range of 200 metres. From a technical point of view, they were 'longbows', since they were obtained from a single piece of wood. The overall height of a Norman bow generally corresponded to that of its user. When not in use, a Norman bow was almost straight; when strung, it was nearly D-shaped in cross-section. Arrowheads could be of three different kinds: blade-shaped, spike-shaped and chisel-shaped. The second model was that specifically designed for combat use, since the other two were employed also for hunting. Each arrowhead was fixed with a tang to its shaft; the latter was made of wood, had feathers applied on the back and was 65–75cm long.

Bibliography

Barraclough ER, *Beyond the Northlands: Viking Voyages and the Old Norse Sagas*, Oxford, University Press, 2016

Brink S, Price NS, *The Viking World*, Routledge, 2008

Cannan F, *Galloglass 1250–1600*, Osprey Publishing, 2010

Cassard JC, *Le Siècle Des Vikings En Bretagne*, Editions Jean-Paul Gisserot, 1996

Cavill P, *Vikings: Fear and Faith*, Zondervan, 2001

D'Amato R, *The Varangian Guard 988–1453*, Osprey Publishing, 2010

Duczko W, *Viking Rus: Studies on the Presence of Scandinavians in Eastern Europe*, Brill, 2004

Franklin S, Shepard J, *The Emergence of Rus, 750–1200*, Longman, 1996

Graham-Campbell J, Hall RA, Jesch J, *Vikings and the Danelaw*, Oxbow, 2001

Harrison M, *Viking Hersir 793–1066*, Osprey Publishing, 1993

Heath I, *Armies of Feudal Europe 1066–1300*, Wargames Research Group, 1989

Heath I, *Armies of the Dark Ages 600–1066*, Wargames Research Group, 1980

Heath I, *Byzantine Armies 886–1118*, Osprey Publishing, 1979

Heath I, *The Vikings*, Osprey Publishing, 1985

Hjardar K, Vegard V, *Vikings at War*, Casemate, 2019

Holman K, *The Northern Conquest: Vikings in Britain and Ireland*, Signal, 2007

Jesch J, *The Scandinavians from the Vendel Period to the Tenth Century: An Ethnographic Perspective*, Boydell, 2002

Jones G, *A History of the Vikings*, Oxford University Press, 1968

Lavelle R, *Alfred's Wars: Sources and Interpretations of Anglo-Saxon Warfare in the Viking Age*, Boydell, 2010

Lindholm D, Nicolle D, *Medieval Scandinavian Armies 1100–1300*, Osprey Publishing, 2003

Logan FD, *The Vikings in History*, Routledge, 1995

Nicolle D, *Armies of Medieval Russia 750–1250*, Osprey Publishing, 1999

Nicolle D, *Arthur and the Anglo-Saxon Wars*, Osprey Publishing, 1984

Oliver N, *The Vikings*, Pegasus, 2013

Williams G, *Weapons of the Viking Warrior*, Osprey Publishing, 2019

Winroth A, *The Age of the Vikings*, Princeton University Press, 2014

Wise T, *Saxon, Viking and Norman*, Osprey Publishing, 1979

Contributors

Hrafn Vaeringi

Hrafn Vaeringi is a renowned combat sports group situated in the United Kingdom, specialising in the portrayal of warriors from the 10th and 11th centuries. With impressive experience in engagements throughout the UK and Europe, the group prides itself on fostering a strong sense of camaraderie and familial bonds among its members. Encouraging individuals to craft their own narratives through the mastery of sword, axe, or spear combat, Hrafn Vaeringi has cultivated a community built on the foundation of martial artistry. Through the art of combat, the group has forged enduring connections and a profound collective identity, akin to that of a tight-knit family. The valour and prowess demonstrated by members both on and off the battlefield have garnered widespread recognition, with the tales of their triumphs resonating far beyond geographical boundaries. Hrafn Vaeringi's fighters are celebrated globally for their remarkable achievements, further solidifying the group's esteemed reputation in the realm of combat sports. As a collective of dedicated and skilled warriors, Hrafn Vaeringi exemplifies the fusion of historical authenticity with a contemporary spirit, embodying the timeless ideals of honour, discipline and kinship. Their unwavering commitment to their craft and their ability to weave captivating narratives through the art of combat serve as testaments to the indelible impact of their endeavours.

Contact
Facebook: www.facebook.com/hrafnvaeringi

Stronghold Re-enactment

Stronghold is a medieval re-enactment society made up of regional groups based around England. Its core shows range from the Battle of Hastings in 1066 to the Battle of Evesham in 1265. Within this time frame, the group focuses on delivering high-quality portrayals of high medieval English life and historical events. These include momentous battles and sieges throughout the period, as well as humble portrayals of life within a travelling encampment or rural village. From fascinating living history activities to entertaining combat displays, Stronghold prides itself on being able to deliver a thoroughly researched and fun medieval experience.

Contact
E-mail: strongholdreenactment@gmail.com
Website: strongholdreenactment.com
Facebook: www.facebook.com/Strongholdreenactment

Compagnie de la Branche Rouge

The Compagnie de la Branche Rouge is a French non-profit historical reenactment group founded in 1999. It showcases a living history museum of 1000AD Europe through the journeys of the Scandinavian Vikings, and the interactions they had with the many cultures they encountered (Frank, Celt, Byzantine, Arabic, Nomadic, Slavic). The group's activities include various crafts such as glasswork (making glass beads such as those found on necklaces), fabric making (weaving, tablet weaving, naalbinding', dyeing, tanning and leatherwork, woodwork and brewing (beer, mead, ash cider and other products obtained with traditional fermentation). The group re-enacts skills of the Viking time, such as combat and military manoeuvres, cooking, table games, physical Viking games and mythology tale-telling. It uses archaeological and historical sources to support its experiments of life in the 10th century and works both as scientific mediators for museums or schools, and as entertainers for city fairs and festivals.

Contact
E-mail: brancherouge@gmail.com
Website: branche-rouge.org
Facebook: www.facebook.com/branche.rouge

Vigamadr

Vigamadr is a French non-profit historical reenactment group founded in 2010. It showcases the travelling camp of Norse fighters and traders from 1000AD. The group's activities include combat display and various crafts. It also presents a travelling long-house to showcase the everyday lifestyle of 10th-century Scandinavians and how housing was set up at the time.

Contact
E-mail: vigamadr@gmail.com
Facebook: www.facebook.com/AssoVigamadr

The Skjaldborg

Founded during 1994 in Omaha (Nebraska), the Skjaldborg is a Viking Age living history group. The group enables enthusiasts who share a passion for the Viking age. With its group motto of 'Many Shields, One Family', the group has created a tight-knit community that strives to help each member improve in kit or combat. Another signature feature is the ability to join and work together on the group mission without a Jarl, king, or other sort of group hierarchy. They are all free men and women coming together without oaths or owed dues. While the group was founded in Omaha, it has since grown to encompass most of the Heartland in the United States, with members and units in Iowa, Missouri, Wisconsin, Minnesota, Illinois, Ohio, and beyond. It is always open to new members. The group has its own Viking trade home in Elk Horn, Iowa. It also helps run, maintain, and build at the Ravensborg Viking Longfort, the first Longfort in America. The Skjaldborg will continue to strive for better combat demonstrations, crafting displays, and contributions to its community and public. Special thanks are due to our photographers: Megan Yenter of Darling Muse Photos, Matt DiGirolamo of 'The Ancient Armory', Kolla Mánadóttir, Daina Faulhaber, Cat Adams, Christian Pearson, Philip Ryan and Amy Studer of the Skjaldborg.

Contact
E-mail: Skjaldborgvikings@gmail.com
Facebook: www.facebook.com/theskjaldborg

Taillefer

Taillefer is a German-based living history project consisting of several individual reenactors who meet up on a regular basis in Germany, Switzerland, France or England to recreate early to high medieval western nobility by focusing mostly on the Norman knight. The biggest and most important event in its yearly schedule is the Battle of Hastings' reenactment.

Contact
Facebook: facebook.com/tailleferlivinghistory
Instagram: www.instagram.com/tailleferlivinghistory

Gunnar

A group based in the Czech Republic and engaged in historical reenactment of Varangians from the year 1000, travelling across Europe in search of glory and wealth. The group consists of around 20 warriors. Its main areas of interest are Sweden and Gotland but, over time, the group has welcomed warriors from other Nordic countries, Eastern steppes, and even one from Ireland. Its primary focus is re-enacting battles and tactics. Each member is a combatant, and the group produces its own equipment and weaponry predominantly in its own workshops. Creations are based on archaeological finds and period practics, consulting with experts in the field. In its 15-year history, the group has participated in more than 100 historical festivals, primarily in the Czech Republic, Poland, Germany, Slovakia, Lithuania and France.

Contact
E-mail: pulsa@vikingove.eu
Website: vikingove.eu
Facebook: facebook.com/profile.php?id=100064741898906

Other books you might like:

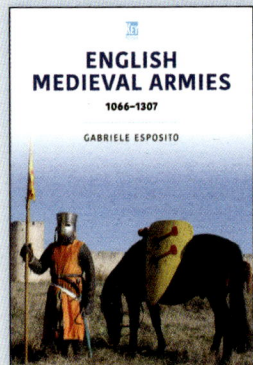
Historic Armies Series, Vol. 1

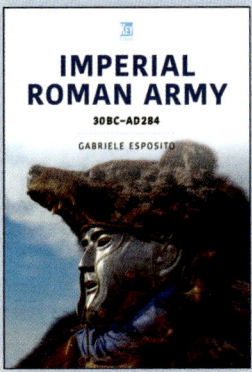
Historic Armies Series, Vol. 2

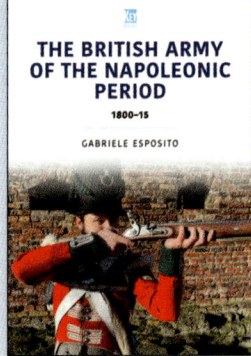
Historic Armies Series, Vol. 3

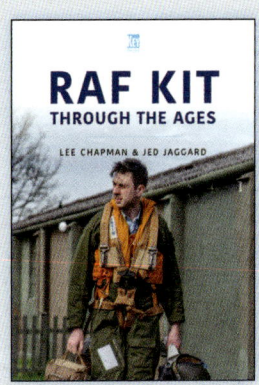

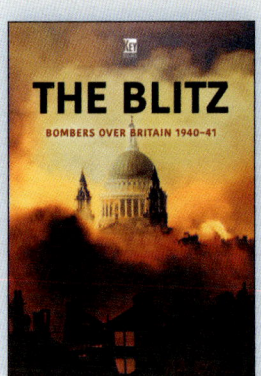

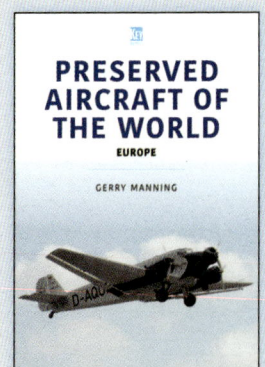

For our full range of titles please visit:
shop.keypublishing.com/books

VIP Book Club

Sign up today and receive
TWO FREE E-BOOKS

Be the first to find out about our forthcoming book releases and receive exclusive offers.

Register now at **keypublishing.com/vip-book-club**

Our VIP Book Club is a 100% spam-free zone, and we will never share your email with anyone else.
You can read our full privacy policy at: privacy.keypublishing.com